Reuben Hunter is an exceptional expositor and faithful pastor. And in *God's Spirit*, he skillfully applies God's Word to the problems of our day. In each chapter, he allows divine truth to speak to human struggle, showing us how God's people are called and enabled to live counter-cultural lives before a watching world and to the glory of God. This book is not only timeless, as the fruit of the Spirit is a subject for which we should all give more attention; but also timely, as we seek to be faithful in a chaotic, divisive, angry, self-centered, and compromising culture. I highly recommend it.

Tony Merida
Pastor, Imago Dei Church, Raleigh, North Carolina
Author, *Love Your Church*

The Bible's primary picture of growth is organic, not technological. But in the age of technology we think we can fix everything and we want things fixed yesterday. We are so often impatient, restless, and distracted. We are reliant on the gods and goods of the world to sedate our minds, improve our bodies, and calm our souls. In our churches we prize size over depth, success instead of suffering, and image more than reality. In all of this we are left malnourished and hollowed out. Reuben Hunter's wonderful book is a life-giving antidote to what ails us. His treatment of the fruit of the Spirit is a beautiful exploration of how God conforms us to the image of His Son. Reuben's love for the God who works so deeply in His people and his love for the reader who needs to learn these truths afresh did me immense good and I'm sure it will you too. I will be making use of this book in many different ways and am profoundly grateful for its richness.

David Gibson
Minister, Trinity Church, Aberdeen

A gem of a little book, at the same time wonderfully encouraging and profoundly challenging. As a pastor, Reuben insightfully discerns both the unfailing promises of God's love for us, Christ's work for us, and the Spirit's work in us, and the messy reality of the daily battles we face which call us to action and not to passivity. The result is a counter-cultural call which offers not only transformation for us as individuals, but for our relationships, and for our society. Recommended.

Dan Strange
Director, Crosslands Forum

Reuben has given us a timely reminder that in a season of chaos where so much has been taken away and our world and our lives have faced 'unprecedented' upheaval, God, by His Spirit, has given us everything we need to live fruitful lives that display the beauty of our Saviour to a world that so desperately needs to see it. I am delighted that what began as a series of pandemic livestream sermons from a pastor to his people has now been put to paper for the benefit of a wider audience.

Athole Rennie
Minister, Grace Church Leith, Edinburgh

We live in a chaotic and disorienting world, but Christians are not left without hope and help. *God's Spirit – The Antidote to Chaos* shows us that the Holy Spirit is at work in the lives of his people, causing us to bear unlikely fruit despite the obstacles we encounter in our flesh and in the world around us. I found it to be an enormously helpful and encouraging book – thoughtful, biblical, practical, hopeful, accessible, and wise. It is an ideal resource for those looking to grow in godliness.

Mike McKinley
Pastor, Sterling Park Baptist Church, Sterling Park, Virginia

Some books can only be written by muddy hands. This is one of those books. Reuben Hunter has not only dug deep in the soil of God's Word, but has toiled to care for the tender plants growing in God's garden, the Church. What emerges is a hope-filled, honest guide to the Fruit of the Spirit that will both comfort and challenge you, whether you're a new shoot or seasoned oak. Pastoral wisdom abounds, simplistic answers pruned. *God's Spirit: The Antidote to Chaos* is the work of a seasoned Pastor-Gardener seeking to water and feed your soul. I warmly commend it to you.

Jonty Rhodes
Minister, Christ Church Central, Leeds, UK

Reuben Hunter writes as he preaches – with warm pastoral concern, keen cultural acumen and a dry sense of humour. This book on Galatians 5:22 is thoughtful, profound, practical and hopeful in a world where the fruit of the Spirit is so needed and in such short supply.

Philip Moore
Network Director, Acts 29 Europe
Pastor, Lagny, Paris

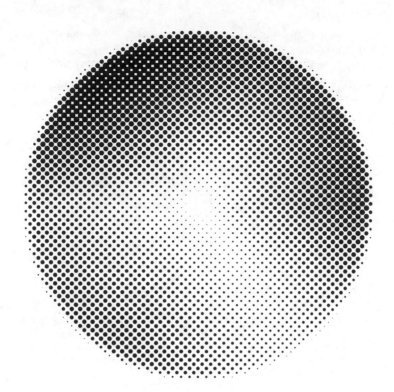

God's Spirit
The Antidote to Chaos

Reuben Hunter

CHRISTIAN
FOCUS

Hardback ISBN 978-1-5271-0839-4
Ebook ISBN 978-1-5271-0908-7

A CIP catalogue record for this book is available from the British Library.

10 9 8 7 6 5 4 3 2 1

Published in 2022
by
Christian Focus Publications Ltd,
Geanies House, Fearn, Ross-shire,
IV20 1TW, Scotland, Great Britain

www.christianfocus.com

Designed by MOOSE77

Printed by Gutenberg, Malta

CONTENTS

We require rules, standards, values – alone and together. We're pack animals, beasts of burden. We must bear a load, to justify our miserable existence. We require routine and tradition. That's order. Order can become excessive, and that's not good, but chaos can swamp us, so we drown – and that is also not good. We need to stay on the straight and narrow path.

JORDAN B. PETERSON, *12 Rules for Life*

It is the Spirit who gives life; the flesh is no help at all. The words that I have spoken to you are spirit and life.

JOHN 6:63

For the law of the Spirit of life has set you free in Christ Jesus from the law of sin and death.

ROMANS 8:2

Now the Lord is the Spirit, and where the Spirit of the Lord is, there is freedom.

2 CORINTHIANS 3:17

For Alan Hunter

ACKNOWLEDGMENTS

There are several people whose influence on and input into this book is right to acknowledge. I first thought of preaching on this topic when I read Jerry Bridges' encouraging and challenging book, *The Fruitful Life*. I reference him directly in some places, but his work is in the background throughout.

I found the idea that we can both cultivate and seek 'counterfeit fruit' a concerning yet very obvious truth. This framed how I pastorally thought about each aspect of the Spirit's work, and it came from the insight repository of Tim Keller, in his *Galatians For You*.

Thanks are also due to Colin Duriez for his editorial work and Rosanna Burton at Christian Focus Publications for her invaluable help throughout this process.

My wife, Louisa, is a constant source of wisdom, insight and encouragement in my ministry and, like anything I say or write, this work is far better for her input.

The good people of Trinity West Church in London first heard this material via a YouTube live stream, and despite the restrictions and the associated frustrations for our worship, they received it with clear evidence of the Spirit's fruit in their lives. I am thankful for the privilege of serving this church family.

PREFACE

Unprecedented.

As the Covid-19 Coronavirus careered around the globe wreaking havoc on civilisation, this was the word on everyone's lips.

People were dying, economies were nosediving, jobs were evaporating, relationships were fracturing, emotions were rising (and falling), political turmoil was fomenting, communities were suffering, governments were creaking, and churches were struggling, and in some cases closing.

This book started life as a series of sermons delivered via video from the Trinity West Church office in Shepherd's Bush, West London. The church family were locked down in their homes; anxiety and anger levels were rising as uncertainty grew all around the world. We were living through a time like no other in most of the congregation's lifetimes as this microscopic virus had taken control of the world, leaving chaos in its wake.

From Wuhan to Washington DC to Wiltshire to Western Australia – we were experiencing a levelling. The foundations of our existence as a human race were being shaken and, as happens in times of stress, things that were previously hidden come to the surface. Like a flatbed lorry with cracks in the chassis, it is only when the pallet of bricks is loaded that the steering starts to go awry. Covid-19 was the pallet of bricks that exposed the cracks in the chassis of our lives and our collective societies.

What does the church do in a time like that? What does the world need in a time like that?

We turned to gurus. The podcast medium exploded during the various lockdowns because of the simplicity of the format. All you needed was a microphone and a laptop and you were all set. It provided a level of connection that we all missed. But the internet has become a growing source of wisdom, especially regarding the struggles of life, for some time. Although he was unwell for most of 2020 and out of the public eye, one of the most influential voices has been Dr Jordan B. Peterson. He published a book called *12 Rules for Life: An Antidote to Chaos* that became a huge best-seller (a second volume has followed with a further twelve rules). Peterson has observed the disintegration of western society, and its effects especially among young men, and his prescription is a return to order and discipline. Tidy your room, stand up straight. His book is full of common-sense wisdom for life in this world. But Peterson is not alone, and this self-help genre has multiplied in the Covid era. Former athletes, soldiers, business experts are passing on the benefits of the discipline they learned in their career.

Another approach we took was to try harder. Former U.S. Navy SEAL Jocko Willinck is another popular internet guru whose approach personifies this. Make your bed, work out, see weakness as a chance to grow. Inevitably there's a lot of common sense in this sort of instruction as well. In the ordered world that God made, many of these rules make for a healthier emotional and physical life. But that's as far as they go.

To live well in this world, even in peacetime, when pandemics have laid down their arms for a while, we need more than 'try harder'. If we want lives that are marked by love, joy and peace, we need more than push through your weakness. If we want to see goodness planted in the soil of our marriages and families, we need more than 'task completion'. What we need is something we can't actually drum up from inside ourselves, however hard we try or however disciplined we become. The truth is, we need someone to come from outside of us to empower us to live the good life. The good life not on my terms but on God's terms. It is His world, and He wants us to live a certain way. But He doesn't just say try harder: He comes to us in the person of His Spirit, to enable us to grow into those people that more closely resemble His Son, the Lord Jesus. This is what the church needs in unprecedented times. It is also what the world needs at any time, and this is what God gives us through the gospel of His Son.

In the chapters that follow there is a reminder and a profound encouragement for the Christian. You have been given the Holy Spirit through faith in Jesus Christ and He is working these beautiful qualities in you. You have the resources you need at your disposal to live a life of love, joy, peace, patience, kindness, goodness, faithfulness, gentleness and self-control. God has gifted this to you through His Son, so look to Him to grow and develop them in you; don't think they can be found anywhere else. But also, alongside the encouragement for the Christian, there is also an invitation to the whole world. Look at the qualities that God grows in those who put their faith in Him. Isn't this the sort of life we are all trying to live? Isn't a life marked by these beautiful qualities what everyone is seeking? We look in all kinds of places to find it, we put ourselves under all kinds of stress trying to achieve it, and yet here is God offering it to us as a gift. Come, and welcome to the good life.

1 The Spirit in a Time of Chaos

2020 will live long in the memory. We've been told that those of us who lived through the Coronavirus pandemic will talk about it, like our grandparents talked about the war. Whether or not that is actually true, only time will tell, but the global disruption has created a bump in our collective roads that means there will be stories to tell for some time to come.

Some will look back with sadness at the passing of a loved one or the loss of a job. For others the memories will be marked by regret, as the grades they needed for university didn't materialise or the pressure of lockdown was the last straw for their already creaking marriage. For some, however, the bump in the road was just what they needed to jolt them into action and they look back with gratitude. The loss of their job was what led to them starting their now successful business. The personal upheaval was the catalyst for finally getting healthy. The sense of fragility was what led them to look up, and to reach out to God.

Some will look back on this time as life-changing; they will thank God for Covid-19, for eternity. Their stories will be told with a smile, because it was during this time that God got their attention and drew them to Jesus Christ.

Many people's lives have taken lots of different turns, some good, some bad. This is the stuff of life. 2020 was a year when people died, got sick, lost their jobs, took opportunities, made money, changed their lives – just like they did in 2019, and will do every year until God calls time on history. What made 2020 different was the intensity of it all. More people were affected more significantly than in other years, but the fundamental realities were the same. We still live in a world that is full of beauty and joy, whilst at the same time cursed because of sin. The requirements that God makes of us remain the same as well. Jesus says in John 15 to abide in Him and bear fruit that will last. He wants us to do this, whether the sun is shining or it feels like the sky is falling in. Because abiding in Jesus is a posture of the heart, we can do it anywhere; because bearing fruit is about our character, we can pursue it anywhere.

Jesus makes this call for fruitfulness just after He has promised to send the Holy Spirit, and this puts what He says in context. Jesus will go to the cross to die for the sin of the world; He will rise again three days later to vindicate Himself as God's Son. Death can't hold Him; He puts death to death. Then having completed this work, He will return to heaven.

But when He does that, He doesn't leave His people to fend for themselves – those who have put their faith in Him and received the salvation He offers. He sends His Spirit to live in them and to enable them to 'be fruitful', as He calls them to be.

The fruitful life flows from the work of God's Holy Spirit at work in believers. That's why we abide in Him: He is the source of this fruit. In

Galatians Chapter 5, the Apostle Paul outlines what it actually looks like: 'But the fruit of the Spirit is love, joy, peace, patience, kindness, goodness, faithfulness, gentleness, self-control' (5:22-23).

This is a beautiful list of qualities. Whatever you believe about the world, about humanity, these are qualities that you admire in others, and you wish you displayed more readily yourself. Who doesn't wish they were more loving, had a deeper peace in their lives, and demonstrated more kindness in their home and with their colleagues? It's not something people tend to say in conversation. 'How are you today?' 'Oh I'm fine. I just wish I was gentler.' But we all wish we embodied these things more than we do.

What Paul's words here show us is that on the one hand, *it is possible*. This is not a list of ideal, desirable but ultimately unattainable qualities. These things can actually characterise our lives. On the other hand, *it is expected* that these qualities will be visible in the life of a Christian.

Such people (in the context of Galatians), having been put right with God through the finished work of Christ, have been brought into the family of God through faith in Christ and nothing else. Those who are heirs of the promise of glory, and have been set free from religious observance, are Paul's longhand for what it means to be 'Christian'. Those are the people to whom the Spirit comes, and in whom He works to bear this fruit.

HEEDING THE CALL

We must start by heeding the call. The section, Galatians 5:13-26, contrasts two possible ways of living your life: two kinds of engine, if you like, that will power how you live. One is the Spirit, and the other, Paul describes as 'the flesh'. And living out of the flesh shows itself in its own grisly list. It covers the …

- Sexual ... sexual immorality, impurity, sensuality,

- Sacred ... idolatry, sorcery,

- Social ... enmity, strife, jealousy, fits of anger, rivalries, dissensions, divisions, envy, drunkenness, orgies ...

Just to make sure he hasn't missed anything, Paul adds 'and things like these' (5:21). The list isn't exhaustive – the flesh always finds new ways of serving itself, inventive ways of attending to its appetites. But when you look down the two lists of qualities, it is obvious that they don't overlap at any point. The fruit of the Spirit stands in stark contrast to the works of the flesh. And Paul calls his hearers to pursue one and not the other. The section is bookended by similar phrases: 'walk by the Spirit ...' (5:16) and 'if we live by the Spirit, let us also keep in step with the Spirit ...' (5:25, Christian Standard Bible).

This is the call. We are to live our lives in step with the Spirit's work. What does that actually mean? A 'Spirit-filled' life, walking by the Spirit, very simply looks like a life shaped by love, joy, peace, patience and so on, and not enmity, jealousy, fits of anger and similar. So Paul expects us to be able to tell if someone is 'Spirit-filled', without knowing or understanding a whole lot about what they think or believe about the world. We should be able to tell by spending time with them. How can you tell if someone is in step with the Spirit? Their lives are full of those lovely qualities. Here we need to clarify several points in order to avoid misunderstanding.

A singular fruit: The word in the original that is translated here as 'fruit' is singular. It isn't *fruits* of the Spirit, like these are different kinds of fruit that the Spirit gives. No, Paul is describing the different characteristics of the singular grace that the Spirit is working in the believer. There is obviously still some value in considering each aspect of this grace – a bit like a gemstone with different facets that reflect the beauty of the stone in slightly different ways. But we mustn't think of them as separate qualities; they come as a whole. If you are a growing Christian, you should be growing in all of these qualities. If that is not the case, it is possible that your joy is just a dispositional happiness, or your patience is just a dispositional dispassion.

A slow-growing fruit: These qualities don't all appear at once. The fruit has to grow and it has to mature, and sometimes the growing season is longer than we would like. We all have a fruit of choice that we particularly enjoy eating. For me it is mangoes. I would like a tree that grew mangoes, and when I picked one another replaced it straight away. That's not how it works, and yet we can often be like this with our expectations for spiritual fruit. We don't want to wait, and when we see it in our lives we want more straight away. We can also be like this with our expectations of others, whether our children, or those in our churches and small groups. But we need patience (of course we do, that's what we're talking about!) because this is not how fruit grows. The important thing about fruit is, if it is growing, you see it, you know it is there – it's the same with spiritual fruit.

So bearing the fruit of the Spirit isn't an optional extra for some elite Christians (there's no such thing!). The Spirit works this fruit in us all, and we should expect to see it. It won't all mature at once and it takes time to grow, but it should be visible. If, when you look at your life honestly, you think the first list is more obvious than the second, there's a problem. What does your life reveal? Impurity? What's your online life like? Dissensions? Anger is cultural currency at the moment. Unless you are outraged on Twitter no one can hear your voice. Drunkenness? How's your drinking? If you are calling yourself a Christian, wherever you see the fruit of the flesh, you must repent of it, and seek the Lord for change. God's people have been called to walk in step with the Spirit.

But that is tough. We need to recognise how difficult heeding this call actually is. Nowhere in Paul's writing does he shy away from this, the flesh and the Spirit. Our natural desires and the work of God, are in conflict with each other.

CHOOSING THE CONFLICT

> For the desires of the flesh are against the Spirit, and the desires of the Spirit are against the flesh, for these are opposed to each other, to keep you from doing the things you want to do (Gal. 5:17).

To put it most simply, when you heed the call, you are choosing conflict. The reason for this is that there is an irreconcilable war being waged between the two sides. This chapter is called 'the Spirit in a time of chaos', and that is only partly a reference to the confusion we are living through in our culture today. It is primarily a description of what it is like to live in the midst of this spiritual war.

Our sinful nature desires the grisly list of qualities, while the Spirit living in us desires that very different kind of fruit. So the Christian will always feel a bit like they are being pulled in multiple directions. But the bottom line is that you have to take a side. I wrote earlier that these two lists do not overlap at any point. If you will be led by the Spirit (v. 18), you must crucify the flesh (v. 24) with its passions and desires.

So it is time to pick a side, to declare our allegiance, to choose for whom we are doing battle. The word that Paul uses is 'crucifixion' – the requirement to put the old nature, the old fleshly man, to death. You have to do this every day, every moment sometimes. The really annoying thing is that it feels like that old man is impossible to kill. He won't stay dead. We think we've beaten him, we turn to walk away and he's there again, whispering in our ear, tempting us to go back.

'Do you want to keep fighting like this? Do you think that's what God has for you? Here's the good life over here. Surely God just wants you to be happy, whatever that involves?'

Paul elsewhere[1] is unmistakably clear: 'put to death'. You simply cannot do a deal with the flesh. There's no treaty that can be struck. So it's a case of choosing the conflict and engaging the enemy again and again and again.

The atheist journalist Ta-Nehisi Coates understands this battle better than many Christians. Writing in the *The Atlantic*, back in 2012, he said this:

> I've been with my spouse for almost fifteen years. In those years I've never been with anyone, but the mother of my son. But that's not because I'm an especially good and true person. In fact, I am wholly in possession of an unimaginably filthy and mongrel mind. But I [also believe in] guard rails.... I don't believe in getting in the moment and then exercising willpower. I believe in avoiding the moment. I believe in being absolutely clear with myself about why I am having a second drink and why I am not. Why I am going to a party and why I am not. I believe that the battle is lost at happy hour, not at the hotel. I am not a good man, but I am prepared to be an honourable one. This is not just true of infidelity, it's true of virtually everything I've ever done in my life. I did not lose seventy pounds through strength of character, goodness, or will power. My character and will angles towards cheesecake, fried chicken, and beer in no particular order. I lost that weight by not fighting a battle on desires terms, but fighting before desire can take effect. There are compacts I have made with myself and with my family. There are other compacts we make with our country and society. I tend

---

1   Colossians 3:5.

to think those compacts work best when we do not flatter ourselves,
when we are fully aware of the animal in us.[2]

If you are going to follow Christ and bear the kind of fruit that He requires, this is the conflict you have to get involved in. For some of us this challenge is more than we can take. We think: 'It's too hard, life shouldn't be this tough … I don't like conflict!' Unfortunately, we don't have a choice. If we want to bear the fruit of God's grace we have to kill the flesh. But Paul closes with a motivation that should inspire even the weariest among us. He highlights the stakes involved. 'I warn you, as I warned you before, that those who do such things will not inherit the kingdom of God' (5:21). It is possible to name the name of Jesus, but still to be living according to the flesh, and when that's the case you forfeit glory. You pass up eternity in God's kingdom. When this is the alternative, you can see it is a battle worth fighting to the death.

It's so important, however, to remember that it's a battle that has already been won on our behalf. Paul, you can see, has been at pains to insist to the Galatians that in Christ they are free – free from the religious requirements of the law – because they have been freed from slavery to sin. The old man, the flesh, doesn't hold them captive any longer. In our lives there are times when it feels like he does, when we feel overwhelmed by temptation or even failure. But when the Spirit lives in us He enables us to fight, and to keep fighting.

If the only power at work in you is your sinful nature, however hard you try, you always fall back into these things. But if God's Spirit is at work, He has dealt sin a fatal blow in the death of Jesus, proving this in the empty tomb. You therefore have been set free to heed this call, and to choose the conflict. You fight with confidence *because* victory is assured.

---

2   Ta-Nehisi Coates 'Violence & The Social Contract: Power Changes People,' *The Atlantic*, Dec. 20, 2012.

2 Love in a Time of Division

Our family has just recently moved house, not ideal in a pandemic but that's how things worked out. We moved to a smaller house which meant that I needed to have a study built in the garden. I managed to get in just before half the nation decided that this was going to be the future, and the company I used was glad to get some work. I talked to the designer on the phone and after several video calls to show him the garden space, he drew up plans and we agreed on a start date. When the carpenters arrived, and got the project under way, one of them asked me how I was planning to use this new shed.

Office?

Man cave?

Gym?

I said it was going to be a study for my work. The obvious next question followed: 'What do you do?' I said 'I pastor a church.' At this point they looked at each other with widening eyes and upward moving eyebrows, and one of them smiled, saying: 'I didn't expect that.' I have to say that I don't mind that response. I am content with the fact that people don't think I look like a minister. But an important question to consider is whether they would have said the same thing by the time they finished the job. After three weeks of being in and around my home, seeing how I treat my family, how I relate to my children, how I treated them when they came to me with problems, or simply just my demeanour with them over the course of the job, would they still have been surprised to hear I was a minister, to hear that I was a Christian?

If you're a Christian, people should be able to tell. Not because of your Bible-verse tattoos or the fish sticker on your car, or because you say you are, or you share the gospel message with people, but because of the quality of your life.

Our passage in Galatians 5 makes that clear. If God's Spirit is at work in you, your life will display these characteristics (22-24). I say they are characteristics. It is important that we don't separate them, but rather think about them as a whole. 'Fruit' here is singular: these are the fruit of what the One Spirit brings about, so that they grow together as one.

We don't actually see one part of the fruit of the Spirit growing without the others. This might come as a surprise because when you think about the quality of a person's life, maybe even your own, it appears that we are stronger in some of these qualities than others. But that could simply be down to our natural temperament (the fruit of nature or nurture), or even natural self-interest (we learned to behave like this because it went well for us when we did). Tim Keller puts it like this:

> Some people are temperamentally gentle and diplomatic (gentle-ness), but the sign that this is not the work of the Holy Spirit is that [they] are not bold and courageous (faithfulness). Because of

what Paul says about the unity of the fruit, this means that this sort of gentleness is not real spiritual humility but just temperamental sweetness.[1]

We mustn't therefore mistake timidity for genuine godliness, or quietness for self-control. We should see evidence of growth in all of these areas.

LOVE

This is why in this book we *are* taking time to drill down to understand what we are actually looking for. As we turn to consider love, we need to start by clearing away a significant amount of confusion. It might just be that confusion on this point is the biggest reason for the problems we see in the world, and in the church.

That might sound like an exaggeration to you. 'Hang on,' you say, 'when I look at the problems in society, what has love got to do with it?' Let me try to show you.

How do people think about love in our culture? That's a book in itself. Here though are three of the most common ways people talk about it.

First, love is random: 'I can't explain it, but I just love him/her. ... I didn't choose this; it chose me.' As a wise man I once heard amusingly put it, 'In this view love is like a ditch!' You didn't notice it, and then you fell in. How many bad decisions have been made because people think that love is this random force that threw them together with someone totally unsuitable? Then, because it randomly again departed, they left that person just as quickly. Society is creaking under the weight of broken marriages that cite this as the reason for the breakup. 'We just fell out of love.' And this is seen as such a

---

1   Keller, *Galatians For You* (Good Book Company, 2013), p. 153.

compelling argument that divorce laws have been adapted to cater for the fallout. Indeed, the social impact of this view of love is felt in all kinds of ways. Real love isn't random.

Second, we think love is overpowering. Here the idea is that when this random force breezes through, you simply can't resist. One of my favourite musicians walked out on his family to be with another artist, who in turn left her family. Sadly, that is not unusual in the entertainment industry. He now says he regrets the hurt that was caused at the time, but with the deepest sincerity he could muster, he said that the love he and this new woman felt was 'bigger than them' and once they had sang together nothing could stop them. He said they couldn't stand in the way of this love, even if they'd tried. That plays well in a film, but there are two broken families that don't agree; two families that wish they had actually loved *them* more than they did.

Then the third way our culture thinks about love is that, if it is real, it is electric. Love requires a powerful physical attraction and if that's not there, it can't be love. If someone doesn't make your heart race when you look at them, it can't be love. If they don't stir your sexual desire, it can't be love. If, at some point, they stop stirring that desire if the electricity burns out, then they can walk away, because with no electricity, there's no love. Who would stay in a loveless relationship?

There are people all across society who are lonely in their singleness because they can't find anyone who delivers this random, overpowering, electricity. They've been told this is what you need for love, and it eludes them. There are also just as many people who have gone into bad relationships because they did feel these things at a point, but they have paid, or are paying, a heavy price for that.

On top of this there is another problem: If this is how you understand love, it doesn't translate to other relationships. If love is random, overpowering and electric, how do you love your parents? Or your children? What does it mean to tell them that you love them? If you can fall out of love in this random way, can you blame children who saw their parents leave each other? Can you think they might walk out on them as well? Maybe the love that came and went in their mum and dad's relationship might do the same in their parental relationship as well.

A love that comes and goes is fairly widespread in the culture. But what about in the church?

It appears that those in the church are just as confused. On the one hand this is no surprise. If this is 'just how it is' in the culture, it is inevitable that these ways of thinking and acting would seem plausible: so much that they seep into the church's thinking as well. In romantic relationships, lots of Christians are waiting for this random, overwhelming, electricity. Because they are working to this misguided standard, it means they both expect too much, and also settle for too little. They want to marry someone who looks the part, and makes them feel a certain way, but when it comes to personal godliness, they will accept a much lower standard.

HOW GOD LOVES

Even more destructive than this, however, is how we understand God's love. If we think love is random, and project that onto God, then it follows that we will live our lives thinking *He* might walk out on us. In the same way that this thing called love came over us, or over someone who expressed it to us, but then left as quickly as it came, what is to say God won't lose interest in me? Going further, what happens when we think that God's love is earned, that we have to perform in order to 'wow' Him in some impressive way? If I can't manage to impress Him, He might cut me loose because I don't measure up.

I have come across a growing number of Christians who lack assurance of God's love for them. While there are always many possible reasons for this, I think one of the main causes is that they think that God loves like the fickle love that they see and experience in the world around them. Plenty of us know enough of the Bible to never say this out loud, but it is what our hearts actually believe. So when we feel like we haven't been good enough – and that is a daily occurrence for the genuine Christian – there's this creeping fear that God might walk out on us. This is a real battle because the air we have breathed from the earliest days teaches us that love is conditional. Parents love us if we behave a certain way, and they reject us if we don't. When I was growing up my mother would often say to me: 'remember Reuben, good things happen to good boys'. She is right. This is how it works. Teachers praise the pupils who behave well and punish those who don't. Sports coaches pick us on their team if we perform, and praise us for doing things well – otherwise we get dropped. In the workplace, whether it is 'Employee of the month' at McDonald's or the City bonus, you earn the praise of others. Even our spouses put conditions on their love for us. We live in a performance-based universe: good things happen to good boys.

God does not love like that. His love is not random, nor subjective, in any way. He loves His children with an unshakeable love. This is because He accepts us: *not* because of what we are able to do for Him, but because He loves us. As this is all a gift of His grace. He promises that He will never leave us nor forsake us. When you put your faith in Jesus Christ, you are secure in God's love.

This is a precious truth that lies at the beating heart of the Christian faith. It is especially precious if you have been hurt in love in the past: if someone has said they loved you, and then gone back on it, maybe even made promises to you. If you are someone for whom 'until death do us part' ended up with 'give me half', I can understand how you might struggle to believe this. But if you want to know just how deep God's love is for you, go to the cross of Jesus Christ. Look at it. Stare into the darkness, the injustice, the agony, the grief, and then you will see there the Son of God taking your sin on Himself. Look again at Jesus who bears your sin away in order that you could receive and experience the deep, deep love of the Father. God went to those lengths for you. You didn't ask Him to, and yet this is the character of His love.

This is the love that is reflected in the Spirit's work in the Christian. Therefore, into the cultural confusion, the Christian is called to love in a particular way. Love that is the fruit of the Spirit will have a particular quality. As I said at the start of this chapter, Spirit-wrought love will be visible. It should be 'showable'. So how will it be seen?

When Jesus summarises the whole Christian ethic, He boils it down to two things. In Mark 12 the religious leaders are trying to figure Him out, perhaps it is better to say *catch* Him out, and look how He responds:

> [O]ne of the scribes came up and heard them disputing with one another, and seeing that he answered them well, asked him, 'Which commandment is the most important of all?' Jesus answered, 'The most important is, "Hear, O Israel: The Lord our God, the Lord is one. And you shall love the Lord your God with all your heart and with all your soul and with all your mind and with all your strength." The second is this: "You shall love your neighbour as yourself. There is no other commandment greater than these."' (Mark 12:28-31).

The love that is worked in the Christian by the Holy Spirit has two parts: love for God and love for neighbour. Jesus is clear that these cannot be separated; the first necessarily leads to the other. You could say they are two sides of the same coin, and this love is really the essence of what it means to be a Christian.

LOVE FOR GOD

> [Y]ou shall love the Lord your God with all your heart and with all your soul and with all your mind and with all your strength (Mark 12:30).

To love with all your heart, soul, mind and strength means to have God at the centre of every aspect of your life. He controls your affections, your intellect, your devotion. At its simplest it means that God takes priority. He gets your best – He doesn't just get squeezed in around the edges of life on your terms. When you love someone you listen to them, want to please them, and want to honour them. It's no different with God.

One of the ways that we demonstrate this love is that we take His word as truth and we obey it, even when the culture doesn't approve. In the verse that follows the 'vine and the branches' section on the fruit-filled life in John 15, Jesus says: 'if the world hates you, keep in mind that it hated me first …' (v. 18).

Why would anyone choose that deal? Who would want to sign up to receive the hatred of the world?

Athanasius, the Early Church Father, stood against the power of the Emperor in his day for the sake of the truth about Jesus. He found himself defending orthodox doctrine in such a way that fell foul of the governing authorities of the day. The story goes that when he was told to recant his views they said, 'Athanasius, the whole world is against you.' To which he replied: 'then I am against the world.' There are plenty of people in the world who get a kick out of being awkward; they seem to get energy from taking the contrary point in any given argument. It was said of a friend of mine that 'he could start a fight in an empty room'. But even the most awkward, contrarian spirit would surely crack when standing before the seat of government. Not if you love God more than anything else. Indeed you will only stand in that way if you love God more than anything else. You will only accept the world's hatred if God means more to you than: the respect of your colleagues; friends or family; the praise of the social media cool-shamer; or the Human Resources department at work.

Just as there are those who enjoy being awkward, there are also some Christians who make a virtue of being offensive. They seem to equate offensiveness with faithfulness to Jesus. Then, when they find themselves being ignored or rejected, they feel content that they are being persecuted for the sake of the gospel. I have on occasion had to break it to these dear souls that they aren't being persecuted for Christ; they are just being annoying. Loving God does not require someone to be obnoxious. It demands that we honour Him even when it's personally costly, and that we don't join in with the culture's cheers at things that dishonour Him.

With that said, chief among the way we demonstrate our love for God is by loving other people. Going back to Jesus in Mark 12, following the command to love God He says there's another command. 'The second is this: "You shall love your neighbour as yourself."'

The Apostle John draws this link most clearly in 1 John 4:20: 'If anyone says, "I love God," and hates his brother, he is a liar; for he who does not love his brother whom he has seen cannot love God whom he has not seen.'

LOVE FOR OTHERS

You can say you love God, and even have really solid theology, but if you don't love others, you don't really love God. What therefore does this require? Random, overwhelming electricity? No, something altogether more meaningful.

Love is a choice

True love is a decision of the heart. In the Bible 'the heart' is the 'inner man', or the will. We sometimes use the word like that when we say that an athlete 'showed real heart'; it has the sense of determination. Putting your mind to it and seeing it through. Anyone who has been married for any length of time will say that this is what they mean when they talk about loving their spouse. Whatever drew them together at the start, as the years go by, with all of the ups and downs, they *choose* to stay together. Two sinful people, living in such close proximity, can and do fall out. What is it that makes them reconcile? It is a choice.

I am well aware that this doesn't sound very Hollywood! It doesn't, but it is actually far better, and here is why. I'd rather have someone tell me they're with me because they have chosen me, rather than because of random chemicals making them feel this way. It is far more comforting to know that someone chooses to love you, rather than that they wake up in the morning wondering what way the romantic wind is blowing. Don't get me wrong: romance is important in marriage; emotion is important too. But you actually choose those as well.

It's the same with relationships in any context: you choose to serve. If we consider the great portrait of love that the Apostle Paul paints in 1 Corinthians 13, each quality is something we choose.

> Love is patient and kind; love does not envy or boast; it is not arrogant or rude. It does not insist on its own way; it is not irritable or resentful; it does not rejoice at wrongdoing, but rejoices with

the truth. Love bears all things, believes all things, hopes all things, endures all things. (vv. 4-7)

These verses are often read at weddings because they remind the bride and groom that in the cut and thrust of their life together, they must choose to forgive, to encourage, and to be generous to each other. Those things don't just happen. Loving someone other than yourself, with the same care you would take for yourself, is a choice you always have to make.

Love is actively other-centred

Loving your spouse, your children, your friend, your church family (the ones you easily get on with, *and* the ones you don't like), your neighbour, even your enemy, requires a choice that leads to activity. You make a choice to move towards them, and you do it for their good, and not just for something you might get from it.

In his study on Galatians 5 Tim Keller talks about what he calls counterfeit versions of each of the qualities[2] the Spirit creates, and the counterfeit version of love is easy to see. At first glance it can look very similar to the real thing, but it comes from a very different source. You see it in the husband who cleans up, listens attentively to his wife when she wants to chat, but does it for a quiet life. You see it when someone does things for others in order that they look good, feel good about themselves, or even for what that person will do for them in return. Doing something for what *you* will get out of it isn't really loving them, it's loving yourself. The kind of love the Spirit works in His people is seen when we choose to actively move towards others for their benefit. And doing it again, again and again.

As is often the case, describing it is easier than doing it. Living a life of love is tough. In fact, if we try to do it in our own strength we

---

2   Timothy Keller, *Galatians For You*, pp. 153-4.

will find that it is actually impossible. So how can we do it? We need to appreciate that we are first of all the recipients of love, before we are able to show it to others. It is only when you know that you have been loved in the most radical way that you are free to love like this yourself.

When you know that God chose to come to earth in the person of Jesus, He chose to set His own privileges aside, in order to fulfil the law of God that we had broken. He chose to go to the cross and suffer, in our place, for our sins. He didn't have to, but He chose all of this. It is when we know that we have received this active other-centred love, completely undeservedly, and that the same Spirit who enabled this selflessness in Jesus is at work in us, then we are free to love as we are called to do.

In the end, our growing in love won't happen if we pursue love as a concept or a thing. It will happen as we pursue Christ.

3 Joy in a Time of Anger

When the scientist Blaise Pascal died, they found a note stitched into his cloak describing how he experienced his conversion to Christianity. It starts:

The year of grace 1654,

Monday, 23 November, feast of St. Clement, pope and martyr, and others in the martyrology. Vigil of St. Chrysogonus, martyr, and others. From about half past ten at night until about half past midnight …[1]

And what follows is an emotional outpouring as he describes what it felt like to see God as God, and to know salvation from sin as something he possessed. And in the middle of it, he explodes: 'Joy, joy, joy, tears of joy.'

If you'd asked Pascal to sum up what it meant to know God, he would have said: joy. It sounds a bit far-fetched for some of us, easy

---

1 Source https://thefederalist.com/2017/11/23/blaise-pascal-saw-november-night-fire-inaugurated-year-grace/ Last accessed December 2021.

to brush off as the overblown emotion of a passionate Frenchman. But in actual fact, the Apostle Paul tells us that 'joy' is the inevitable fruit of the Spirit of God at work in our lives.

So why are we sceptical? The critics of Christianity latch onto this sort of thing with a roll of the eye: 'Oh spare me the fakeness! The happy clappy nonsense, the cheesy smiles and relentless positivity! No, thanks.' They are cynical because they have their eyes open in the real world. Sickness, disease and death are not things to rejoice in. A cursory read of the BBC News homepage shows how messed up things are, so how can someone be joyful in a world like this? Some scepticism says, 'This can't be real.'

But the scepticism isn't reserved for cynical opponents of Christianity. Perhaps you *are* a Christian and you're thinking, 'Oh spare *me* the fakeness! I believe the gospel and I've put my faith in Jesus. But it's not like this in my experience.' Your Christian life is one tough day after another. And you're not all that keen on the relentless positivity either!

Wherever you're coming at this from, I want to suggest that if you are cynical about the possibility of your life being marked in significant ways by joy, it is because you've fallen for something I'm going to call, 'The happiness lie'.

We use the words 'happiness' and 'joy' interchangeably; we think they're the same things. So, when our culture tells us, as it so forcefully does, that happiness is what life is all about, and we should do whatever it takes to be happy, then it defines what happiness involves, we come unstuck. When life is about happiness, and happiness is found in being a particular kind of person who possesses certain things, and when you can't, or don't, meet that standard, you are not happy. Because you are not happy, you don't have any joy. Our culture understands this. Therefore books with titles like 'The Happiness Myth', and 'The Happiness Trap', seeking to offer their own solutions, sell by the million.

We need to understand, therefore, the happiness lie. On the one side, thinking that life is all about happiness, but then on the other thinking that, when we're not happy, there's nothing else. This is mistaken because happiness is tied to our circumstances. When those circumstances suit us we are happy, when they don't we aren't. Ask anyone who orders the food they like from the menu, or sips a cold drink on a hot day, or closes on the purchase of a house they wanted to buy. In that moment they are happy, and so it follows that it is entirely possible to be very happy in life, and not be a Christian. C. S. Lewis said:

> I have an elderly acquaintance of about eighty, who has lived a life
> of unbroken selfishness and self-admiration from the earliest years,
> and is, more or less, I regret to say, one of the happiest men I know.
> From a moral point of view it is very difficult.[2]

But this is completely dependent on getting what you want, and so it is inherently fragile. This was one of the biggest lessons we were taught by the Covid Pandemic. People have had what they want taken from them, and their happiness has evaporated. The phone lines to mental health charities were ringing off the hook because people were not able to work out what to do when they weren't happy, and were restricted from doing anything that might change that.

We fall for the happiness lie when we settle for happiness as our life goal. It's misleading because happiness is fragile and because there is in fact something better: something that runs deeper, because it doesn't depend on you getting what you want. It is the joy, uniquely Christian, that comes from the Holy Spirit.

---

2   C. S. Lewis, *God in the Dock* (Grand Rapids, Michigan: Eerdmans, 1972), p. 48.

Throughout the New Testament we see examples of people rejoicing despite their trying personal circumstances. Acts 13:52 describes the disciples as being 'filled with joy and with the Holy Spirit' as they brought the gospel message to different places. During these trips they often encountered opposition and were very badly treated, I'm quite sure they weren't always happy, but still they rejoiced. When Paul writes to the Philippians, he's under house arrest, chained to the prison guard. People on the outside whom he thought were partners in ministry are making his life very difficult. It is quite likely that he was not all that happy, and yet the letter is full of joy. Happiness is fine, but joy is way better. But what is it, exactly, that we are looking for?

A DEFINITION

Spirit-wrought joy is a contented delight of the soul, that flows from finding God to be supremely beautiful, and enables us to trust in His word and His work.

Joy is a contentment of the soul. Deep in the heart of your being, there is a sense that whatever is going on, however hard the winds of suffering are blowing, you are secure and the world is in good hands. But you can't just drum up this sort of experience in your own strength. You can't buy it with more possessions, or more provision for the future.

In the middle of the Covid pandemic there was a high-profile legal case in London between the Hollywood actor Johnny Depp and the publisher of *The Sun* newspaper. The Hollywood star sued *The Sun*'s publisher for libel after a 2018 column, by its executive editor Dan Wootton, described him as a 'wife beater'. Depp and his ex-wife, Amber Heard, went in and out of court each day and the media scrum pored over every sordid detail they could find. What emerged as the weeks went by was that Depp – although very successful, very wealthy, and very widely loved – had a chaotic personal life. He came across as a restless rather than a joyful soul.

That case is a lived example of the happiness lie. We are told that if you get these things you'll be happy; but the happiness always stops. A joyful soul is created by the Holy Spirit: only He can bring this about. He does it by opening our eyes to the beauty of God. We exist in the hands of a supremely majestic Creator, who didn't just start the world running and leave us to make the best of it. He sustains our world moment by moment, giving us life and breath, and everything we have. We possess all that we have as a gift from His hand.

We don't just see God's beauty and infinite worth, but the Spirit also causes us to trust in God's word. Apart from the Spirit, the Bible is just words on a page. You might find a nice moral tale or two in there that reads well alongside Aesop's Fables. You might dig a bit deeper and appreciate the literary skill of the authors. You might keep a Bible on the shelf in case you are ever asked to say a few wise words on special occasions. But apart from the Spirit, that is as high as you go, the Bible simply takes its place alongside Shakespeare or Seamus Heaney.

But when God's Spirit opens your eyes and ears and you see this as the living word of the living God, it changes everything. God speaks to you personally. He explains the world, the human condition, and ultimately, He shows us the Lord Jesus Christ. In the end, the Bible is a book about Jesus – in the Old Testament He is promised, in the Gospels He is revealed, in the Acts He is taught, in the epistles He is explained, and in Revelation He is expected.[3] We come to see and understand this because the Spirit reveals it to us.

---

3 For a fuller treatment of this idea see Alec Motyer, *Look to the Rock: Old Testament Background to Our Understanding of Christ* (Westmont, IL: IVP, 1996).

The Spirit also makes Christ real in our experience. The historic facts around the person and work of Jesus are: being born in Nazareth to Mary and Joseph, lived a life of perfect obedience to God, was executed using crucifixion by Roman soldiers, and three days later He rose from the tomb. That all happened, it is historically attested. It is possible however to know the facts and to be completely unmoved – there are historians who know every detail, but who remain fervent atheists. It is only when the Spirit gives us eyes to see, and ears to hear, that these details become personally real. Only when the Spirit opens our eyes to our need of a Saviour, and convinces us that Jesus is that Saviour, do we put our lives in His hands.

It is the Spirit who enables us to put our faith in Jesus, and who unites us to Him; we are said to be 'in Him', and because being in Christ is being in the Son, who is beloved of the Father, we are able to rest in God's providence – to trust His work in our lives and in the world.

Spirit-wrought joy is a contented delight of the soul, that flows from finding God to be supremely beautiful, and enables us to trust in His word and His work.

That is a definition and explanation of Christian joy, but we must press this into the corners of our lives a bit more to see how it plays out in practice. It is important to say at this point that the Spirit is at work in different ways in different people's lives; but if you have put your faith in Jesus Christ for salvation, these following five statements are true of you, and you can assert them confidently about your life:

- God the Father loves me
- God the Son died for me
- God the Spirit lives in me
- He's working all things together for good

- I'm on my way to glory

In many ways, this is a succinct summary of what it means to be a Christian. It is the basis of how the Spirit creates a life of joy in the believer because it tells us the following:

WE ARE FORGIVEN, SO GUILT IS GONE

Some of us like to think of our past as if we were going through customs, the green lane at the airport: *nothing to declare*! But we know we're kidding ourselves. We might wish it was the case, but the truth is often very different. If we're honest we agree with the opening of Alfred Lord Tennyson's poem 'Remorse', when it says:

> 'Oh! 'tis a fearful thing to glance back on the gloom of misspent years: what shadowy forms of guilt advance, and fill me with a thousand fears!'

The things we've said and the things we've done, never mind the things we've thought. I can be happily going about the normal things of life when out of nowhere I will remember something I said or did even decades ago, and I will be filled with shame. Do you ever feel that way? When those memories return or those thoughts rise up, we want someone or something to deal with the sense of guilt. The truth is that the offence we might have caused to other people is nothing compared to our offence against God.

To sin against a Holy God has been described as cosmic treason, and so our greatest guilt is before Him. Yet in Christ that guilt and shame is taken away at the cross. Among the sweetest words in the Bible is Paul's declaration in Romans 8:1 that 'there is therefore now no condemnation for those who are in Christ Jesus'.

So we can confidently sing those well-known words penned by Charitie Lees Bancroft,[4]

> *When Satan tempts me to despair*
> *And tells me of the guilt within*
> *Upward I look, and see Him there*
> *who made an end to all my sin.*

Forgiven. Guilt is gone. Joy.

WE ARE LOVED, SO INSECURITY IS GONE

So many of the decisions we make in any given week are driven by a desire to be well thought of or accepted and admired by a particular person or group of people. This informs the way we dress, the way we speak, the way we behave in general. But it also means we're vulnerable to the fickle opinions of those people. When we need the approval or love of other people we are very insecure. But when your eyes are opened to who God is, and the acceptance that He grants you in Christ, you realise you are loved by the only person whose opinion matters.

When God says: 'I accept you, not on the basis of what you look like, or what you can do for me ... but because of Christ,' this sets us free. It liberates us like nothing else, because it means you don't need the approval of anyone else. No one else can influence your eternity, so what does their opinion matter?

WE ARE SAFE, SO FEAR IS GONE

The Apostle Peter writes:

> Blessed be the God and Father of our Lord Jesus Christ! According to his great mercy, he has caused us to be born again to a living

---

4 'Before the Throne of God Above,' 1863.

hope through the resurrection of Jesus Christ from the dead, to an inheritance that is imperishable, undefiled, and unfading, kept in heaven for you, who by God's power are being guarded through faith for a salvation ready to be revealed in the last time. In this you rejoice ... (1 Pet. 1:3-6).

If the universe is a series of random forces, nothing is certain. If it is created and sustained by the majestic, triune God, then it's a very different proposition. If you know that even in the hard times, God is in control, and in His infinite wisdom, He is working all things, all of them, together for good, we are ultimately safe. He is with us leading us through the trials of life, and He will ensure that we make it all the way to our inheritance in glory.

When you know that one day, everything sad will come untrue and that the future is secure, all of the fears that grip our world dissolve. We are safe, fear is gone, and there is abundant joy.

None of this depends on circumstances. It's got nothing to do with what you have or don't have. Forgiveness, love, safety – these are the things that our culture is desperately hungry to find, and yet God gives it to all who trust in Jesus Christ as a gift, and the Spirit applies it to our lives. To the extent that you know this – the extent to which you believe that you are free from guilt, insecurity and fear – is the extent to which the Spirit will flood your life with joy.

So that's the challenge. You see, if we're going to refuse the happiness lie, and enjoy God's fatherly love and all that flows from that, we will have to fight for it.

THE FIGHT

The Spirit doesn't work on a blank canvas. He works in hearts and minds that are conflicted and turned in on themselves, and want to take control and pursue joy on our own terms. This could be in a religious context, by keeping the rules and being self-righteous like in the Galatian church that Paul is writing to, or it could simply be by pursuing whatever the culture tells us will deliver the good life. We therefore need to break that habit. The only way to do this is to fight to submit your will to God's will. The only way you'll do that is to see the greater joy in it all.

This is like what Jesus did when He went to the cross. He embraced all of that suffering for the 'joy that was set before him'. He embraced obedience to God's plan because that was where ultimate joy lay. This is why He said, as He faced the cross, 'not my will, but yours, be done'. That is the fight that every Christian must take up. To say to God every day: 'not my ideas of what I need to be happy, but your will in every aspect of my life'. It is when we do that with sincere hearts that the power of God – the same power that enabled Jesus, the power of the Spirit – enables us. He doesn't take us out of the fight, but He empowers us in it, and He sees us through.

Again we are back where we started with the realisation that the pursuit of Spirit-worked joy will be a battle. We engage the fight, however, because of what is promised when we do: not the fleeting pleasures that this life offers, but deep, soul-satisfying joy.

4 Peace in a Time of Discord

Here in the West, we have never had so much. We have privileges that would have been beyond our grandparents' wildest dreams. This hit home to me recently when I saw a photo online from the 1980s. The man in the picture had a video camera on one shoulder, a radio tape player on the other, he was wearing headphones and on a table in front of him there was a personal stereo, a calculator, a VHS video player, a fax machine and a digital minidisk player. The caption below said: 'Now you can carry all this in your pocket.' If you own a smart phone, they say there is more technology in that, than what was required to take a rocket to the moon. In the developed world we have never had so much, and yet we have never been so restless.

WE ARE ANXIOUS

Thankfully, many of the traditional causes of anxiety and depression are in decline, things like poverty, poor health, and such. But there are new ways for fear and frustration to take hold of our lives; new ways in which anxiety is triggered. Our culture's obsession with a particular kind of 'success' has created real problems. *Medical News Today* published a study back in the 1990s that found that people who 'pursued money, looks, and status were more likely to be anxious and depressed'. It seems like we haven't learned the lesson, because the *pursuit of money, looks and status* is the reason why many Londoners get up in the morning.

The reason these things lead to anxiety is obvious; they are fragile. We get some, we're anxious for more, we lose some, and we start to wobble. It is well documented that the prescription of sedative drugs and anti-anxiety medication has sky-rocketed over the last thirty years, and part of that explosion is because the age people are being medicated for anxiety is dropping all the time.

WE ARE ANGRY

We have seen this in London with the amount of protesting there has been in recent years. But protests are not new. They have always existed as a way of the people having their voice heard by the powers that be. What is new is the level of anger that we are seeing at these protests. When the media do their vox pops there is a tangible sense that blood is up and tempers are on edge. 'Why are you protesting?' … 'Injustice?' … 'Where?' … 'Everywhere!'

It is also the case that the general language in the media feels increasingly aggressive. Conflict makes headlines which sells column inches, so there's a benefit in stoking the fires a little. Politics has never been known for its kindness, but from local councils to Parliament itself the tone of communication seems to have more spite now than it once did. Now the phenomenon of social media doesn't just enable this spiteful and angry communication to be more widespread more quickly, but there's also something about the format that seems to encourage people to say things they wouldn't say face to face. In fact, I think Twitter's tagline could be: 'Enmity, strife, fits of anger, rivalries, dissensions, divisions … when it happens, it happens best on Twitter.'

We see it on a small scale too. On the roads, in our homes, in our relationships, tempers are short, offence is taken easily, lots of us are on the edge a lot of the time. Then a global pandemic is thrown in! This has taken anxiety and anger to another level. We are anxious about our health, and angry with the people who don't seem to care. Anxious about the future, angry about the government's handling of the lockdown. Anxious about our jobs, angry with our employers for cutting our pay. Anxious about everything, angry with anyone who doesn't think like us, or do what we want. If there was ever a time that we needed the peace that the Spirit gives – inner contentment and rest – it is now. We can't create peace in our own strength, the sales of anxiety and depression medication show that. Paul however says that when the Spirit of God is at work in your life, peace is something you should expect to see. How is this possible? Well, it starts by Him creating peace with God.

PEACE WITH GOD

The human heart is naturally at war with God. You might think that sounds extreme: 'Don't be daft, I'm not at war with God. I just don't bother with Him.' But it doesn't work like that, because of who God is. The God of the Bible is Lord, King of the cosmos, and so it is right that we all acknowledge that. As those He has made, He owns us and we should then give Him the honour He deserves. So when we don't do that, however politely, however passive our rejection of Him is, we are at odds with Him.

There wasn't a time when we consciously chose this. This is how we are born. This is why the Bible uses words like 'alienation' and 'hostility' to describe our relationship with Him. All of our problems start here. It's like the builder getting his foundation wrong. If his measurements are even slightly off, the problem at the source means the whole thing is out of kilter. That's us when it comes to living lives marked by peace: discord, at source, means that discord in other areas of life is inevitable.

> We are not at peace with others because we are not at peace with ourselves, and we are not at peace with ourselves because we are not at peace with God (Thomas Merton).[1]

So we need to get the foundation right, and that only happens through faith in Jesus Christ. 'Therefore, since we have been justified by faith, we have peace with God through our Lord Jesus Christ' (Rom. 5:1).

When we put our faith in Jesus, when we hand over the control of our lives to Him, all the hostility between us and our Maker ceases. It works like this. All of the anger God feels, quite rightly, for the way we have lived in His world on our terms, and all of the penalty that our sin requires, falls on Jesus at the cross. When we see Him being nailed up, even though He had done nothing wrong, we see a man going there for us. When He does that, justice is done and God's anger is turned away.

If you have put your faith in Jesus Christ, your punishment was taken in Him, your penalty was paid in Him, and so hostilities between you and God, cease. We are reconciled. We have peace, and what this means is that instead of being opposed to us, God is now

---

1   www.brainyquote.com/quotes/thomas_merton_399785 Last accessed December 2021.

for us. Instead of leaving us to make the best we can of this life, His Spirit now lives in us to help us, so we're not doing it on our own. Instead of seeing the struggles as meaningless, He in fact is working even them for our good. Instead of uncertainty about the future, God is keeping us for glory.

You can see why peace *with* God is the foundation from which all other peace will flow. When you know that the King of the cosmos is on your side, whatever is going on, it changes how you view and experience *everything*. It is then from this foundation that the Spirit then creates what we might call the peace of God.

THE PEACE OF GOD

Before He returned to His Father, Jesus promised to send His Spirit, and in the section in John 14 where He talks about this, He says to His disciples: 'Peace I leave with you; my peace I give to you' (v. 27).

So the same peace that characterised Jesus' earthly life is what the Spirit gives to those who trust Him. Just as Jesus' inner life was one of contentment and confidence in His Father, and just as He only sought conflict with others when it was right, and did so without sin, so this peace is what the Spirit creates in the life of the believer.

Can you believe this? Does this describe your experience in the day to day of life? If you're anything like me, that is unlikely. We struggle with inner conflict and turmoil, and when those things take hold of us they overflow into conflict with others. We need, therefore, to find a way to get peace, both in ourselves and with others.

IN OURSELVES

We do that first by reminding ourselves of what God has done for us, and praying and trusting ourselves to His fatherly care. That sounds, however, just like the sort of glib truism that an out-of-touch preacher would say from the detached heights of his ivory tower. It's not that easy. Life is hard, and the battle to trust God is very real.

When I think about this, I keep being surprised by how things often go down. When a big crisis hits, that's when I expect people to get scared and start to crumble emotionally. But often, it is in the crisis that they turn to the Lord, and find they experience His grace and peace. It is the fairly trivial or mundane things – like a never ending to-do list, or something someone said or did – that we chew over in our mind, that actually unsettles us and robs us of our peace. What things are most likely to upset your peace?

Is it, perhaps, that someone has wronged you and you allow resentment to fester? Or is it that they haven't wronged you, but you just think they're getting a better deal in life, and you're envious? Or can you simply not let a grudge go? When your friends try to tell you to let it go, you can't. 'It's the principle!' you say. 'It's about right and wrong.' That might be true. I'm not suggesting that we just overlook injustice where we see or experience it. But that is precisely the kind of mindset that takes away our peace.

We are restless. Our anxiety and anger are allowed to take control, because we don't believe that our Heavenly Father cares for us. We don't trust that He can take care of what is going on around us. In many cases we can affirm all the right theology: 'Yes, God loves me. Jesus died to reconcile me to Him. The Spirit lives in me; He's working all of the circumstances of life together for good. I'm secure in all of this, and will make it safely to glory. I will defend to the death, that beautiful theology. But ...' And that 'but' is our unbelief that creates the discord.

The same God who knows the number of hairs on your head, and who holds the whole world in His hands, knows what He is doing in your life. It is when you trust Him – not just bringing some bland and generic prayers that you think sound Christian – I mean trust Him with *your* life, with all of *your* struggles, *your* temptations, *your* doubts and fears, *your* sin, thanking Him for *your* blessings and His kindness in *your* life – then your heart and mind will experience the peace that the Spirit brings. This is what the Apostle Paul tells the Philippians:

> Rejoice in the Lord always; again I will say, Rejoice. Let your reasonableness be known to everyone. The Lord is at hand; do not be anxious about anything, but in everything by prayer and supplication with thanksgiving let your requests be made known to God. And the peace of God, which surpasses all understanding, will guard your hearts and your minds in Christ Jesus (4:4-7).

It is interesting that he doesn't say 'go and be at peace'. He makes it clear that peace is the fruit of other things. So, it seems to work like this: if we pursue joy, trust the Lord, bring *everything* to Him in prayer and thanksgiving, then peace will follow. Indeed, Jerry Bridges reminds us of the centrality of prayer in this when he says: 'The great antidote to anxiety is to come to God in prayer. We are to pray about everything. Nothing is too big for him to handle, and nothing is too small to escape his attention.'[2]

The thing that is promised when we trust ourselves to God in prayer, especially in times of trouble, isn't an end to those trials, but peace.

At this point you might say, 'I follow the thread, and that sounds great, but it's not like this for me. I've been praying about [x] for years and I'm still agitated, anxious and angry.' Do remember that we're talking about the fruit of the Spirit. He's the One who works it in our lives, so ask Him directly: 'Lord, give me this peace, please. Make it

---

2 Jerry Bridges, *The Fruitful Life* (NavPress, 2018), p. 77.

possible for me to get through the day without worrying, or getting angry, or …,' and push on in prayer until He answers.

That is how we cultivate peace within: but how does this work out in our relationships?

WITH OTHERS

We have strife in our relationships for the same reasons: when we don't get what we want, whether that is respect, or love, or some kind of appreciation; and when another person doesn't treat us the way we want to be treated, we get anxious or angry, or just bent out of shape in some way. But if you know, in the depths of your being, that whatever that person thinks of you, God loves you. The Lord of all the earth is for you, and He showed this by sending His precious Son to die for you. This reframes how you view that situation. When you think about how God loves and accepts you, what does the opinion of someone else matter?

If someone is treating you badly and making your life very difficult, when you know that God has given you His Spirit to help you to endure, and He is working this suffering for some good end, you can trust Him. Even when that person is sinning against you, in the gospel you have the resources not to retaliate: even to forgive, and to rest in the goodness of God. I'm not suggesting for a moment that this is easy, but it is possible, because that is what Jesus did when He was so badly treated. During His earthly life Jesus did all that He did, not in His own divine strength, but in dependence on the Holy Spirit. He was rejected, suffered and loved His enemies, and prayed for His persecutors in the power of the Spirit. Remember, Jesus said: 'Peace I leave with you; *my* peace I give to you.' The peace the Spirit gives is the peace of Christ, so even in conflict, you can know that same peace.

The place where we should see this play out most of all is in the context of the local church. We know that churches can fall into conflicts and divisions. This happens anywhere that sinners are brought together, so Paul says in Romans 12: 'As far as it depends on you, live peaceably with all ...' (v. 18) and in chapter 14 'Make every effort to do what leads to peace.'[3] But it is important to know that we can do this because of the Spirit's work. When you appreciate that in Christ you have been adopted into the same family, sharing the same heavenly Father, participating in the same Spirit, you can be wronged and you can forgive, because love covers a multitude of sins. Also, you can admit you were wrong, and seek peace with others that you have offended as well. The church of Jesus Christ is the one place on earth where discord can be meaningfully dealt with, and relational peace can be a real thing. So don't withdraw. Peace isn't the same thing as indifference, or coolness, or distance. It is what follows forgiveness and reconciliation.

The fruit of the Spirit in your life, therefore, will be seen when you pursue peace in your relationships with others. If there is discord between you and someone else, especially in the church, take the initiative to put things right – whether you have wronged, or been wronged, doesn't matter – pursue peace. Unresolved conflict is toxic in any environment, but it can spread through a church like cancer. Like cancer the longer it is left untreated, the worse it gets. The best time to pursue peace with others is now. Our world is anxious and angry, and the church often follows their lead. But we don't need to, because if you know Jesus, His Spirit brings us peace *with* God, and the peace *of* God.

---

3   Romans 14:19, New International Version.

5 Patience in a Time of Instant Everything

Imagine having to wait ten minutes for an Uber, or thirty minutes for a Deliveroo food delivery. Think how you feel when you click through an online order, and are told that your purchase will take three to five days to be delivered. However, it has to be next day, or same day, or one hour. I will admit to having walked out of a shop empty handed because I heard the words, 'unexpected item in bagging area'. Resolving this would have meant waiting for the lady with the magic codes, and that would have taken more time than I cared to give.

According to an online article in Forbes, 'compared to two years ago, smartphone users are 50 per cent more likely to expect the ability to purchase something in real time ... According to Google, search interest for "open now" has tripled in the past two years while searches for "store hours" have subsequently dropped. The implication? Customers who act right now expect brands to cater to their intent right now, quickly and relevantly addressing their needs that very moment.'[1]

Imagine in that moment when you want to know something, anything, you had to find a book and read it. Or the way it feels when you 'Google it' and you're faced with the great evil known as 'buffering'. Imagine having to save up for something rather than getting it now on credit, or insisting your children save up for something you could easily afford to buy them. It is confusing to our modern ears that you would delay gratification like this. We live in an on-demand world where we can have what we want, when we want it, and this sets higher and higher standards for our expectations. In fact, impatience has become something of a virtue, because we think it is completely reasonable to get angry if we have to wait for anything. We live in a generation that has what Simon Sinek calls 'an institutionalised sense of impatience'.[2] As we come, therefore, to consider the Spirit's work of creating patience in His people, here is where the Christian can, and should, stand out in our day. As we look at our culture and see how ingrained impatience has become, it feels like this quality of patience is something only God could create. But the good news is, He does create it, and we can see this by looking at the three main areas in which impatience tends to grow – with circumstances, with others, and with God.

WITH CIRCUMSTANCES

Our world is broken and hard things happen in a broken world, and there may be a million things, things that just seem to happen

---

1 https://www.forbes.com/sites/briansolis/2017/11/20/impatience-is-a-virtue-how-the-on-demand-economy-is-making-mobile-consumers-impatient/?sh=5eb8d4c344ca Accessed 23/07/20

2 I heard this online in one of his ubiquitous talks.

without any direct involvement from other people, on any given day, that irritate us and make us impatient.

It could be a fault on the train line on your commute, road-works when you're in a hurry, a pandemic that messes with all your plans, or an automated message: 'If your call is about the fact that we took hundreds of pounds from your account, please press 2.' It might also be that you hate your job and you can't find a new one. Perhaps you are waiting for the solicitor, or the estate agent to call you back, or you are being told that the contract or information is 'in transit'. You just want whatever it is to be sorted out, *now*.

We get impatient to have the things that we want, to change our circumstances, or to have what we feel we deserve. When it comes to possessions, if we can't afford them, we get credit because we simply can't wait!

If we press a bit deeper than that, we can get particularly impatient when we *suffer* in some way. Why is this sickness not lifting? Why can I not get over this injury? Loneliness, anxiety, depression, grief: I'm sick of all these, why won't they go away?

In lots of ways this impatience is understandable. But if we could change perspective so that we were able to ask, *What is the Spirit doing in these circumstances?* – we would see that He is cultivating the fruit of patience. In so much of our day-to-day impatience, the problem is that control has been taken from us. As God takes control out of our hands, we have to wait on Him. But while patience is a good thing, it's not an end in itself. Listen to Paul in Romans 5:3-5:

> [W]e rejoice in our sufferings, knowing that suffering produces endurance [patience], and endurance produces character, and character produces hope, and hope does not put us to shame, because God's love has been poured into our hearts through the Holy Spirit who has been given to us.

Hard circumstances, even the hardest that involve suffering, are designed to create patience, and that patience produces, in turn, the other delightful qualities of character, and hope. When you meet someone who's life circumstances are tough, and they are patiently trusting the Lord, that has come from the Spirit. But someone in that situation is always someone whose character you will admire and who will have their focus on the glory to come. Especially if that suffering seems to have no real point – as when you see a young person with a debilitating illness and are left asking 'why?' Or your marriage is miserable, and you can't seem to change it. When your circumstances are that hard, the faithfulness of God to His promises, and the liberation and joy that the Last Day promises, are precious to you. In hard or frustrating circumstances, the Spirit is growing patience in you by challenging your illusion of control, by cultivating hope for the world to come, and by growing you in maturity.

WITH OTHERS

The second area where we are tempted toward impatience is with other people. Maybe they are the cause of our suffering, in as much as their behaviour is directly affecting us in a negative way. They provoke us, and when they say 'that' thing, or act in 'that' way, it just gets under our skin, and our blood begins to rise a degree or two in temperature. Maybe it is just their shortcomings, but it still frustrates the life out of us. It may be the bad driver on the road in front of you, your friend who never turns up on time, or the people in the flat upstairs who make so much noise. The closer you are to someone the more this gets to you: their personal hygiene, their eating habits, their sense of humour. 'More often than not, it is the unconscious action of some family member whose irritating habit is magnified because of close daily association.'[3]

---

3   Bridges, p. 90.

Impatience can raise its head in every kind of relationship: in the home, with the children, amongst friends, in the church family. In particular, it seems to happen a lot in the workplace. While our first thought might go to the employee, feeling this way about the difficult boss, jokes abound, where the difficult boss getting his or her comeuppance is the punchline. But it is just as likely to be true for the person in authority over others. This may be when you are trying to motivate a passive member of the team, or you are relying on them for work that they don't deliver, or don't deliver when you need it. The temptation is to give them 'the hairdryer' treatment, and certain aspects of leadership-culture still celebrate this kind of response. What does patience look like in these cases?

To answer this question we need to start with the different words that the New Testament translates as 'patience', and this will help us to see how the Spirit does something slightly different in each case. He cultivates and grows our patience in different ways.

LONG-SUFFERING

The first word that is translated as patience in our English Bibles is literally 'long-suffering'. This is the quality that we need when it comes to being unjustly treated by others. The Spirit therefore cultivates our ability to suffer a long time when we're mistreated, without getting bitter or resentful. He helps us to trust in the justice of God, and He does this because it is the example of Jesus. This was what Peter said to slaves that were harshly treated by their masters. He urged them to consider Jesus: 'When he was reviled, he did not revile in return; when he suffered, he did not threaten, but continued entrusting himself to him who judges justly' (1 Pet. 2:23).

When our blood begins to boil, and we feel our back straighten, and hands tingle, ready to retaliate against being wronged, the right response is to trust ourselves to God, who judges justly. God will not make any mistakes when His judgement comes, and we can rest in that, even when our grievance is real, and the pursuit of earthly, temporal justice is a right and good thing to do. We find this so hard, but the truth is, we struggle because we don't think God will do as good a job as we would.

> One of the thoughts that most disturbs a suffering Christian who has not learned patience is this issue of justice. He is concerned that his tormentor will escape justice, that he will not receive the punishment he deserves. The patient Christian who suffers leaves this issue in the hands of God.[4]

As a pastor I have seen the fruit of long-suffering in people's lives on several occasions and it is a deeply beautiful thing. I can think of a couple who lost a baby at the final stages of pregnancy, in large part because of medical negligence. They were advised that had they wanted to, they could have taken the hospital to court, which would have led to a huge compensation pay out, and effectively ended the doctor's career. They chose not to take that path, but instead to leave the whole sorry situation in the hands of God. Only the Holy Spirit can lead someone to act in this way; it's certainly not 'natural'. But what has been particularly beautiful about this situation, is the effect this couple's patient trust in the Lord's sovereign care has had on their ability to heal from this tragedy. Because they left the horror of the whole thing with the One who judges justly, they have been liberated from bitterness, and their lives are shot through with joy. The sadness remains, and with every lost birthday the pain returns, but you couldn't know this couple without wishing you had some of the joy that marks

---

4 Bridges, p. 87.

their lives. Only the Holy Spirit can create this kind of fruit, and it is wonderful to see in action.

We also need to be long-suffering in the face of *provocation*. When we are being pushed and prodded again and again by Mr or Mrs Thorninflesh, we need the Spirit to work. In this case He takes us beyond Jesus' example, to grasp the patient character of God. When our hearts are taken up with how patient God is with us, we are patient with others, even the most tedious and infuriating. Think about it. The offence that we might feel when someone doesn't afford us the respect we are due, is as nothing compared to the offence caused to God when rebellious people despise His authority, and show contempt for His word. That is what we do time and again by nature. We don't even need to consciously think about it, it just comes to us, it's instinctive. Yet God is 'slow to anger, abounding in steadfast love … forgiving wickedness, rebellion and sin'. The key to displaying patience when we are provoked is to reflect deeply on this long-suffering patience, of God towards us. He never loses His temper with His children. He never rashly turns His back on us. He never says: 'What's wrong with you? Why are you doing these same disrespectful things again …?'

When we lose our patience because we've been provoked in some way, we forget God's enduring patience with us. We want to punish that person; God wants to forgive. We want to exercise our authority; God is eager to exercise His patience. We want to hurt; God wants to love. Godly patience doesn't overlook the provocations of others; it simply seeks to respond to them in the right, God-like, slow-to-anger, kind of way. When you resist the desire to satisfy your heightened emotions, therefore, and instead bear with this annoying person, the Spirit is bearing the fruit of patience in your life. When you resist the desire to exact retribution whether with words or actions, praying instead for repentance and reconciliation, the Spirit is bearing the fruit of patience in your life.

FORBEARANCE

When it comes to patience with the faults and failings of others, the best word is forbearance. Paul uses this in Ephesians 4:1-3: '… walk in a manner worthy of the calling to which you have been called, with all humility and gentleness, with patience [forbearance], bearing with one another in love, eager to maintain the unity of the Spirit in the bond of peace.'

Literally the word means 'put up with' or 'tolerate', and when this is worked in us by the Spirit, our forbearance isn't given grudgingly. It is done with grace and love, because it seeks the higher good of forgiveness and unity. It is also concerned with cultivating the sort of relational peace we looked at in the last chapter.

It should be said that Spirit-worked forbearance doesn't rule out confronting people when they do stupid things, or when they have annoying habits. There is a place for correction in the Christian life. But the way you will be able to tell if that correction comes from the Spirit, is that it is done with the right attitude. It won't come from pride, superiority or overflowing frustration; it won't have that *'for goodness sake would you stop* …' tone, that belies exasperation. It will come instead from love that desires the welfare and good of that person. The patient forbearing friend, spouse, or colleague will come with a more conciliatory tone: 'Can I talk to you about the way you speak to me sometimes?'

Our culture doesn't celebrate the quiet humility of those who forbear others in their folly. In fact, patient people are often misunderstood as passive, or even a bit weak. You can see how it happens. Patient people are in control of their anger, and they usually have a tight rein on their tongue. They don't therefore stand out, especially when they find themselves around those who are quick to speak. In addition, we have created a category of acceptable, or even celebrated, anger. So we laugh at the stand-up comic whose routine revolves around his unravelling temper. When our friend retells the story of his office contretemps, where his parting shot was a harsh put down, we nod in affirmation of his machismo. There's no story when he tries to tell us that when his colleague wound him up, he only nodded, smiled and walked away without a word. No one laughs when we talk about how, when we were provoked by someone, we reflected on the forbearance of God, deciding not to retaliate – and found it very liberating. Patience isn't very 'cool', but it is mature, and it belies a God-given strength that our culture of short fuses and sharp tongues desperately needs.

WITH GOD

This area where we are tempted to impatience is with God. If you have been a Christian for any time at all, you don't need me to tell you that our plans and God's are often on different timetables! Even when we don't quite say it straight out, we are often impatient with Him to do what *we* want. In some cases, the thing that we want is a good thing, in line with His word – the salvation of a loved one, the provision of a husband or wife, for some suffering to end, for a long-standing problem to be resolved – and the fact that He doesn't answer only serves to increase the frustration. He makes us wait, sometimes all the way to glory, and our big question is, why? Why does God do this to us?

This is a perennial question both for Christians and for those looking into the faith, and it is not one I will answer adequately here. But there are several points to make that should inform how we think about the situation. For starters, if God answered every prayer we prayed, by giving us what we asked for, it would probably destroy us. If we're honest with ourselves, we know that this is the case. Is this not why, when successful people are interviewed, they are often asked, 'What would you tell your younger self?' The point of the question is that hindsight and experience teach us, that things we thought, desired, or even cared about, ten or twenty years ago, look very different now. The country music legend Garth Brooks, in a typically sentimental way, sang about this in his song 'Unanswered Prayers'. If you don't know the song, it's about the singer and his wife bumping into his old girlfriend from high school. It talks about how back then he dreamed of marrying this girl. But all these years later he's glad it didn't happen, and he thanks God for unanswered prayer in this area.

> She wasn't quite the angel that I remembered in my
>   dreams
> And I could tell that time had changed me
> In her eyes too it seemed
> We tried to talk about the old days
> There wasn't much we could recall
> I guess the Lord knows what he's doin' after all [5]

The spiritual fruit of patience recognises that, not just in sentimental country songs, but in our trials and struggles that God has good purposes for us in 'unanswered' prayers.

It also recognises that the Lord is forcing us to depend on Him more fully and so pressing us into a deeper intimacy with Him. We learn very little about ourselves and about God when we always get what we want in life. But when God frustrates our desires, we discover how shallow our prayers are, how little we really trust Him,

---

5 Garth Brooks, 'Unanswered Prayers', 1990.

and how when He is all that we have, we realise that He is all that we need. This sounds better when we say it to others than when we have to live it in our own experience. But ask anyone who has lost their health, their soulmate, has been betrayed by those closest to them – someone who has had nowhere else to turn but God – and they will tell you about good thing after good thing that they learned or experienced in that time.

Obviously, there is some overlap in these three categories. This is because God is sovereign over our circumstances, and the lives of other people, so our impatience with those things is in the end impatience with God. So He isn't giving us the life we want, in whatever way that works out. When people don't treat us the way they should, however that happens: when you don't give up and walk away; become resentful towards God; or resort to going through the motions while really your heart is as hard as stone. But when you patiently trust Him to bring His purposes to pass, pushing in to depend on Him more deeply, that is the work of the Spirit. He is cultivating the fruit of patience in your life. The lesson we must learn, therefore, is that we don't resist the frustrations God puts in our way. This is because His Spirit in our lives is growing patience – that in turn creates character and hope, remember.

When the culture trains you to expect instant everything in life, cultivating patience is hard, and sometimes so is receiving the Spirit's ways of cultivating it. But as we look forward to glory, however far in the future that is for us, we need this patience. As the writer to the Hebrews put it: 'We do not want you to become lazy, but to imitate those who *through faith and patience* inherit what has been promised' (6:12, NIV). Only those patient make it to the end, so let me encourage you to take confidence in your frustrations that God is equipping you by His Spirit with what you need to get there.

6 Kindness and Goodness in a Time of Selfishness

When people talk about you, it could be your friends or your colleagues, or perhaps just your wider family when you are not around, what would they say? Perhaps a better way to frame the question is to fast forward to the end: how will you be remembered? David Brooks in his book, *The Road to Character*, talks about the difference between resumé virtues and eulogy virtues. Our resumé virtues are the things we put on a CV: our talents and accomplishments. Eulogy virtues are the things that they say about you after you're gone. What will those who know you best say about you on that day?

I ponder that question from time to time, and wonder, but I know this. If your life bears the fruit of the Spirit, that we're considering in this chapter, people *will* remember, and that will be the focus of their eulogy. Kindness and goodness stand out like very little else, especially against the backdrop of our contemporary western culture. There's an undeniable ugliness in our public discourse, and there's an anger and selfishness that seem to prevail, especially in that window into the human soul that is social media. We saw remarkable acts of kindness during the pandemic as nurses cared for the sick, and communities came together to care for the lonely and isolated. But we also saw anger, that was obviously being held in check, burst through the cracks as people felt the pressure that Covid brought into their lives. All this means that when you see kindness and goodness, it stands out.

As we continue to consider this list of the fruit that is borne by the Holy Spirit, as we abide in (that is, stay close to) Jesus, I am taking kindness and goodness together. We often use the terms interchangeably, and there isn't much to distinguish them – but they are distinct. One way to consider the distinction is to see that goodness is kindness in action. Think, therefore, about kindness as the sincere desire to do good for another person, and goodness as acting on that desire to serve. Kindness is the awareness of a person's need; goodness is acting to help them. Kindness in fact is the inner disposition to care; goodness is the external expression of that. So they go together, and as I said, they are a clear reflection of the character of Jesus. This comes together nicely in the letter to Titus, where Paul speaks about the way God works in saving His people, and he says that we were once lost. 'But when the goodness and loving kindness of God our Saviour [Christ] appeared, he saved us ...' (Titus 3:4-5), not by our own works but by His grace.

Paul uses his words synonymously, but the point is that the kindness of Jesus is *seen*; it is visible, in His action to save us. He is kind *to* us by doing good *for* us. Once again this means that as we wonder what these qualities will look like, Jesus is our example. The Spirit who cultivates fruit in our lives, is the Spirit of Christ: He is the same Spirit Jesus relied on, during His earthly ministry.

Jesus was kind. His heart was moved towards those who had need – the marginalised, the poor, those who were, for whatever reason, cut off from God.

Think about that well-known story in the Gospels, where Jesus is on His way somewhere, and the crowds are following Him: lots of people walking, pushing in on Him. He then stops, saying, 'wait, someone touched me!' Lots of people were touching Him. But a particular person had touched Him in a particular way. It was a woman with a health problem that had destroyed her life. She had tried every kind of medication or alternative therapy, and bankrupted herself in the process. She was now hopeless and wanted to be healed. She believed that this man could do that.

She slipped through the crowd and thought that just touching His cloak would be enough. Jesus could have brushed it off. There was plenty on His mind; lots of things He needed to do. He didn't heal everybody. But He stopped, and wanted to know who had touched Him. She made herself known, an unclean outcast. Jesus' heart was moved. So He acted to heal her. Kindness was seen in goodness.

How will you see the fruit of kindness in your life? In the good deeds that you do? Later Paul says that, 'as we have opportunity, let us do good to everyone, especially to those who are of the household of faith' (Gal. 6:10). That is only possible if we have a kind heart. Now we need to say at this point that kindness and goodness are not to be confused with 'niceness'. Niceness has become something of a virtue in Christianity, but it isn't a fruit of the Spirit. On the one hand, it's a bit of a nothing word. If I was to ask you to define 'niceness' you would inevitably use other words like 'kind' in the description. But often what is really meant is that someone is polite or mannerly, or will never offend. But on the other hand, 'niceness' is a subjective category. Other people decide if someone is nice or not according to their own categories. Often things like being truthful, or being willing to disagree with someone, stand in the way of being thought of as nice. That's okay. Politeness is good, manners are important. I'm not suggesting that we should seek to be impolite or boorish. But kindness and goodness might – indeed they likely will – require you to be thought of as 'not very nice' from time to time.

Let me give an example: If you are not a Christian and I say to you, 'God made you, and the world you live in belongs to Him. The things you enjoy in life were given by Him. But because you don't acknowledge that, and thank Him accordingly, you are in sin. And the truth is, He is angry about that, and if you go on rejecting Him, you will be cut off from His goodness for eternity.' I'm actually being kind by telling you that. Anyone who warns another person of impending danger is doing a good thing, and there is no greater danger than facing the judgement of God. But in British culture today, that sort of approach in conversation isn't seen as very nice. Doing good to other people requires Christians to push beyond nice. It requires us to push *through* nice in order to get to good. When danger looms for someone, the very kind person doesn't just warn them, but tells them how they can avoid the danger. They will tell that person that whilst we *have* sinned against God – and that's uncomfortable to admit – 'He sent His Son to die and rise in order to deal with your sin. If you turn and put your faith in Jesus, you will be forgiven, cleansed, and reconciled to the God who made you.'

So being thought a 'nice' person shouldn't be our goal, rather it should be a kind person who therefore does good to others: that is the fruit of the Spirit. In fact, Paul says that this is the very goal of our salvation: 'For by grace you have been saved through faith. And this is not your own doing; it is the gift of God, not a result of works, so that no one may boast. For we are his workmanship, created in

Christ Jesus *for good works*, which God prepared beforehand, that we should walk in them' (Eph. 2: 8-10).

What, therefore, will this look like in practice? It could work out in all kinds of specific ways depending on your life circumstances, but here is what Spirit-worked goodness might look like in three common areas.

IN THE FAMILY

Starting with the family, embodying the fruit of goodness, means living out God's design for your stage and status. If we simplify things, and go back to the beginning of the story, we hear God's command to Adam and Eve to multiply, to fill and subdue the earth.[1] This is God's design for humans as humanity: therefore doing good, according to God's original design, means establishing godly families. To get to that point will mean that a man will pursue a woman, not for his own ends, to satisfy his desires, but to become his wife. They will then order their relationship according to God's word. The husband accordingly will assume the sacrificial leadership that God calls husbands to embrace, while his wife will respond by respecting and following his leadership.[2] They will then seek to have children and raise them to know, love and serve the Lord Jesus Christ.[3] This is an incredibly demanding task, not one anyone can accomplish without the help of the Holy Spirit – but the calling is straightforward. Doing good, for society and for the sake of the gospel, should involve getting married and having families.

I should say that not everyone will do this. God does set some people apart for singleness, and there are some who won't have

---

1 Genesis 1:28.

2 Ephesians 5:22-33.

3 Ephesians 6:4.

children. Speaking of God's normative pattern in the Bible doesn't rule out, or diminish, those who don't conform to the pattern. It is important to say that singleness is not a lesser state for the Christian. Indeed, there are some cases where it is preferable.[4] The Apostle Paul labours in 1 Corinthians to celebrate it, as this is where God has some people in the Corinthian church. It is important, however, that the church doesn't take her lead from the culture, more than the Bible, in this area.

Goodness according to God's design requires us to calibrate our expectations for life, to His word, and raising godly families takes time and effort, and can't be done on the fly. If you aren't available to your children, in order to lead them spiritually, you should reconsider your priorities, especially when they are young. I heard a wise, older Christian liken children to freshly poured concrete, where there is a limited time to move, and shape things, before it is permanently set. Parents, and fathers in particular, addressed in Ephesians 6:4, need to be available, and involved in the younger years. This will mean opening the Bible with the family regularly, leading them in prayer and engaging the children with the things of God in the ordinariness of day-to-day life. This is what was intended in the Old Testament law: '… these words that I command you today shall be on your heart. You shall teach them diligently to your children, and shall talk of them when you sit in your house, and when you walk by the way, and when you lie down, and when you rise' (Deut. 6:6-7).

This is at the heart of what it looks like to bear the fruit of goodness in the family context. Paul even emphasises this when he talks about how the church should treat widows, in 1 Timothy 5. Goodness is very clear. 'Let a widow be enrolled if she is not less than

---

4   1 Corinthians 7:6ff.

sixty years of age, having been the wife of one husband, and having a reputation for good works: if she has brought up children, has shown hospitality, has washed the feet of the saints, has cared for the afflicted, and has devoted herself to every good work' (1 Tim. 5: 9-10).

A widow should be materially supported by the church if her life displays the fruit of her Christian faith; that is, if it is marked by good works. What are the good works she is known for? Paul says that a commitment to raising children – filling and subduing the earth – is one of the fundamental ways this will be seen. If you are, therefore, committed to the godly nurture of your children – the painstaking, heart-wrenching, often thankless task of raising godly children – that is the fruit of the Spirit in your life. However tough you're finding it, keep going in the strength that God supplies, knowing that you're doing the work He has given you, and it is good.

IN THE CHURCH FAMILY

Moving beyond the 'small-F' family, we should also consider what goodness looks like in the 'large-F' church family. This will be seen in things like hospitality,[5] serving others and caring for the needy.[6] In a healthy church community this will be going on in all kinds of ordinary ways without any fuss. In the church that I serve I see this going on in very practical ways: people open their homes to others freely; sharing what they have; putting someone on their car insurance to help them get around more easily; hosting people who need somewhere to stay for a while; helping provide lifts and meals when babies are born; and giving money anonymously to those they know are struggling. These are just the examples that I know about. There is a whole lot more going on in unseen ways, as people

---

5 1 Peter 4:9.

6 Matthew 25:42-46.

bearing the fruit of goodness do their works in secret, just as Jesus commanded. This is when you can tell the Spirit is the One who is driving things, because these acts of service aren't about people getting praise for themselves. Rather, they are about meeting needs, providing care, and just doing good because it is the right thing to do. When you see it, it is a lovely thing to behold.

IN THE WORLD

The third area where this goodness will be seen is in the wider world. When Paul talks about care 'for the afflicted' in 1 Timothy 5 (v. 10), he doesn't just mean inside the community of the church. I said earlier that Galatians 6:10 tells us to 'do good to everyone, and especially those who are of the household of faith'. The 'especially' here means we prioritise, but we don't ignore needs in the community or the world around us. Historically it has been the church that has led the way in social initiatives: caring for the homeless; helping the alien and stranger; looking after widows and orphans; and bringing basic kindness to those that society has overlooked. In a day when the State has taken responsibility for lots of these things, it is important that the church doesn't stop seeking to do good to all. Despite the growing government influence in social care in the U.K., we still have problems with homelessness, with traumatised asylum seekers who need care, and with poverty – to name a few obvious areas where our Spirit-worked kindness and goodness will make a difference to the lives of others.

These qualities will look different for different people at different times, but here are three ways that they might be expressed in your life:

Firstly, your hospitality will be extended to people who aren't just like you. I'm thinking of Jesus' words in Luke 14 about not having dinner parties for people who will return the favour. There is absolutely nothing wrong with having dinner parties with people like you – friends are a gift from the Lord, and none of us should feel guilty about having them. But when the Spirit bears the fruit of goodness in our lives, it will be seen in our having people in our lives who don't look and sound like us. It will be apparent in us spending time with people who don't benefit us in any way.

Secondly, doing good means serving the Lord where you are now. The globalism of our culture has given us this sense that we can change the world from our kitchen table. Many of us have grand plans to leave our mark on society and that might be fine. Ambition in itself isn't a bad thing. Nothing significant would ever have happened if it wasn't for the ambition of those who pushed their ideas, and drove the change. But it is often the case that our grand plans prevent us from doing the ordinary, mundane things that are right in front of us – the things God has put in our lap. The way you leave a lasting spiritual mark is by doing what's in front of you *now*, to the glory of God. You change the world by being faithful to God in the work He has given *you*. Raise *your* children, and fire them as arrows into a time that you won't see. Serve the poor in *your* street, care for the needs of *your* church family, love the people *you* have been given to love. This is where your goodness will be seen and experienced.

Thirdly, and above all, seeking the good of others requires us to seek their greatest good, which is their eternal good. The story of history is very simple: God is real, Christ is our only hope, and eternity is a very long time. Kindness, therefore, that shows itself in goodness, seeks to hold Christ out to the people around us. We will do this in different ways according to our context, and how we are wired, but we will do it. As I said earlier, some people won't think this is nice, but it is always kind and good.

When time has passed and we look back, whether as church communities or as individuals, people won't remember a whole lot about us. They won't be as impressed by the 'resumé virtues' as we might think. They won't remember the sermons from church, the soundness of our theology, or our rhetorical gifts in reasoning about the Christian faith. But they will remember our kindness and goodness. Isn't that what it's like as you think about your parents, that teacher at school, that sports coach, or that person who told you about Jesus? As you think about their names now, as you imagine the expression on their faces, as maybe you can even hear the tone of their voice, what do you remember? He was a kind man; she was a good lady. As the Spirit works in our lives this is what people will remember about us.

7 Faithfulness in a Time of Pressure to Compromise

It might be the marriage that endures sickness and strife and is still strong after fifty years. It might be the friend who always turns up no matter what. It might be the person who stands with someone when others depart, even when it costs them professionally or personally to do so. Wherever we see it, and especially if we experience it ourselves, we really admire faithfulness. True faithfulness is a beautiful thing.

I have a friend who was once the subject of an article in one of our national newspapers. The article was critical, spiteful, and full of factual errors, but that was not the worst thing about the situation. What my friend found hardest was how quickly friends and colleagues distanced themselves from him. Even though the episode had happened many years before, he still found it hard to talk about how lonely and isolated this made him feel. But just as painful as the memory of those who turned away from him, was the warmth and affection he felt for those who stood by him. We were just chatting in a busy London café, but as he described the faithful few who put their heads above the parapet to support and defend him, and as he talked about this loyalty and courage, I could feel myself getting goosebumps. Faithfulness is very attractive, so it's no surprise that we find it on the list of the Spirit's work in the believer's life. 'The fruit of the Spirit is … faithfulness.'

The word means loyalty, trustworthiness, and reliability. The reason it is on this list is that these are the characteristics of God Himself. He is faithful to Himself and to His promises, so when God the Holy Spirit is at work in our lives, He makes us like Him, so we bear the fruit of faithfulness as we grow to image God.

As I have said throughout this study, this list of qualities isn't another law. It is not a list of things we need to achieve in order to please God. These are the qualities that the Spirit of God brings about in the life of someone who is abiding in Christ: the man or woman, boy or girl, who is trusting and walking closely with Jesus. This book is primarily, therefore, about knowing what, if you call yourself a Christian, you should see in your life. It's the same again in this chapter. What will we see when the fruit of faithfulness is growing in us? Some of what that means will be obvious, but I also want to point out areas where to be faithful may require us to grow.

FAITHFULNESS TO GOD

Spirit-worked faithfulness will be seen, first, in our faithfulness to God. At the obvious level, this is seen in unswerving loyalty to His word. God has made Himself known in the Bible, and He has told us what He requires of us there. Hence you see the fruit of faithfulness when someone opens their Bible, reads it, and does what it says, no matter what anyone else might think. They will also be someone who is marked by a commitment to meaningful prayer. Often today, talk about faithfulness and loyalty relates to an office – the Queen, or the President – or to an inanimate object, such as the flag, or the nation. But when it comes to God, the faithful person knows that their commitment is relational; they are faithful to a person. And so like any relationship they express their commitment through communicating. Now we need to grasp what this actually looks like, because for many of us I believe we think of prayer a bit like the drive-through at McDonald's. So, we speak, we think there's someone at the other end, and if we want something we have to go through a strange, disembodied transaction, hoping they will give us what we've asked for. Prayer shouldn't be like that; we should liken it to a child speaking to their father, or spouses talking, or friends communicating. You don't just ask for things in those relationships in a transactional way. You're relating together in ways that shape your understanding of that person, and help you to know them and love them more deeply.

Then, of course, faithfulness to God will be seen in our desire to tell others about Him. He has tasked His church to go into all the world and tell people about His Son, the Lord Jesus. In our culture at the minute, we don't need to look too far to see all kinds of expressions of anger and conflict. It feels very close a lot of the time. Where does this come from? It comes from the rebellion that exists in every human heart towards God, their Maker. Despite His glory and goodness, we turn our backs on Him, and set our lives up on our terms. What does He do in return? He sends His Son to take the punishment we deserve for living in this way, on Himself – dying for sin, in our place. Then He rises again to new life, and grants that very life to any and all who turn to Him in faith. That's the hope for the world, our world. If we will be faithful to God, we will tell our world that this is the whole point of their existence – to find salvation and hope in Jesus Christ.

If you have been a Christian for any length of time, I suspect you know most of this already. When it comes to talking about faithfulness, this is what you would expect. But it's fairly general. That's right, because the specifics of faithfulness will look different for different people, depending on their situation and life stage. However, there are some areas in this cultural moment where the Christian's faithfulness is being particularly tested, and where the temptation to compromise is very strong. A clear-sighted sage once said:

> If I profess with the loudest voice and clearest exposition, every portion of the truth of God except precisely that little point which the world and the devil are at that moment attacking, then I am not confessing Christ, however boldly I may be professing Christ. Where the battle rages, there the loyalty of the soldier is tested.[1]

There are several areas where we currently see that the 'battle is raging' for Christians; here are two very obvious ones.

GENDER AND SEXUALITY

God created men and He created women. He created us all equal, but different along the lines of gender and sex. Some people are born in a category that has become known as 'intersex' but those are few and their condition is treated as a medical problem. This means that at a fundamental level boys should be raised to become masculine men, and girls should be raised to become feminine women. This understanding of our humanity would have been widely held in British culture even as recently as late 1990s. Indeed, as Carl Trueman has said in his book, *The Rise and Triumph of the Modern Self*,[2] 'the phrase "I am a man trapped in a woman's body" would have made

---

1 The source of this quote is unknown. For many years it has been attributed to Martin Luther, but it doesn't appear to be in any of his works.

2 Carl R. Trueman, *The Rise And Triumph of the Modern Self* (Crossway, 2020).

no sense to my grandfather's generation and would have been dismissed as a joke.'

Alongside this, there is the issue of sexual intercourse. God created sex and stated clearly how it is to be enjoyed – one man and one woman within the marriage covenant. Again, while it would be wrong to suggest that there was a time when sexual immorality was absent from the culture, it wasn't that long ago when this was the ideal that people sought. They married with an eye to the benefit that marriage has for the fabric of society, not just their own desires, and sex was reserved for the marriage.

Things have changed with an alarming speed over the last two decades, and this means Christians are on the back foot. American cultural commentator Aaron Renn has developed a helpful taxonomy for assessing this cultural shift that distinguishes between positive, neutral and negative worlds. The Christian no longer lives in a positive world, where their views are popular and widely promoted. Or even a neutral world, where their views are tolerated, and they are largely left alone to believe what they want and act in line with those beliefs. We now live in the negative world which Renn summarises like this: 'In this world, being a Christian is a social negative, especially in high status positions. Christianity in many ways is seen as undermining the social good. Traditional norms are expressly repudiated.'[3]

What this means is that if you say that there are two genders, and sex belongs in marriage in our culture, you're a hater, a 'phobe' of some sort, and you'll be hounded on social media in order to be cancelled. Holding those views today have put your job, livelihood, reputation and even safety on the line. But faithfulness to God

---

3   Aaron Renn, The Masculinist #13, The Lost World of American Evangelicalism, https://www.aaronrenn.com/wp-content/uploads/2018/03/The-Masculinist-13-The-Lost-World-of-American-Evangelicalism.pdf Accessed 24.05.21.

requires us to stand up for what He says on these things. True human flourishing follows the Maker's design – that's what we are saying. But when that is shouted down, faithfulness will stand.

FREEDOM

This is another area where Christians are under pressure. First, in relation to the government. The Bible teaches that God has established three estates, or institutions, in society – the family, the church and the government – and they each have specific responsibilities. Government, according to 1 Peter 2, is meant to punish those who do evil and praise those who do good. Put simply, this means their responsibility is to protect life, freedom, and property and Christians are to be law-abiding people. We are to honour the rule of law and in many ways be model citizens in the local community; this will commend the gospel.

But where the State demands loyalty beyond its God-given remit, we need to be aware of this so that we don't unthinkingly put the State over God. In the book of Acts, therefore, when Peter is told by the governing authorities to stop preaching the gospel, he says: 'no'. And his reason is that he must honour God before any other ruler. The more libertarian among us need to remember that Romans 13 commands us to obey the governing authorities. It is just as important, however, for the rest of us to remember that governments can overreach, and be aware of what well-known writer-editor, Rod Dreher, calls 'soft totalitarianism'.[4] Faithfulness to God requires us to honour Him above men.

The second area where this is relevant is in relation to free speech and 'cancel culture'. We are rightly concerned when the

---

4   Dreher develops a very cogent case for this in his recent book *Live Not By Lies: A Manual for Christian Dissidents* (New York: Sentinel, 2020)

State silences its citizens, but we should be equally concerned when mobs gather to do the same. We have seen a rise in something called deplatforming, where people who have been invited to speak, usually at a university campus, are 'uninvited'. We see it when BigTech delete Twitter accounts. We have also seen a rise in recent times in online groups crying for blood when someone's opinions don't fit their prevailing narrative of choice. Christians need to remember that their beliefs don't fit the prevailing narrative, and so freedom to say the things the Bible says, without fear of being cancelled, is something we should prize. Faithfulness is seen when we engage in reasonable dialogue, and defend the rights of people to say things, even things we may find offensive, rather than joining in, as so many uninformed Christians tend to do, online or otherwise, to cancel these opinions – or even just to stand back and applaud while others do the 'dirty' work.

There are other areas, but these two are currently live, while the contemporary church has decided that not rocking the boat is the best approach. We would rather not be saying the awkward thing, perhaps particularly because we want to stay onside with the cultural gatekeepers. Sadly, my fear is that we are compromised as a result.

The spiritual fruit of faithfulness, however, is seen most clearly when to be loyal to God is hard and unpopular, when the 'soldier's loyalty is tested'. There was a long-running legal case in the media that came to a head in 2020, that brought these two prickly cultural issues together for a Christian family who owned a bakery in Northern Ireland. Ashers Bakery cancelled an order and refunded the money of a man who wanted them to bake him a cake with a slogan written on it that they didn't feel their Christian faith allowed them to promote. They decided that they couldn't glorify something that God says is not to be glorified. With no prejudice to the individual who placed the order, as a privately owned business they had the right to decline the order. But because the text on the cake concerned gay marriage, the customer alleged discrimination. Because the story was big, as a version of 'bigoted Christians deny gay man his rights,' the media jumped into it with both feet.

As a private business, Ashers should be free to choose who they do or don't serve – case closed. But as the equalities commissioner got involved, and the court case ran into months and years, what was interesting was how many Christians joined the waves of criticism for the stance this family had taken. Indeed, every time I saw the young couple on television news making their statements, it was striking both how out of step with the culture they looked and sounded, but also just how great the sweep of opposition against them had become. I can't imagine how it must have felt to be vilified the way they were: to be the focus of everyone's coffee-chatter; to have their faces on the front page of national newspapers; and even to be scorned by stand-up comedians. In fact, they could have conceded at any point just to get back to a normal life, but they didn't. They were faithful.

FAITHFULNESS TO OTHERS

The spiritual fruit of faithfulness is seen in our faithfulness to God, but it will also be expressed in faithfulness to others. These two categories overlap, as part of being faithful to God is being faithful to others; but this will be seen in the relationships we have. It is apparent in the person who keeps their word, and in the workplace is known to be reliable; the sort of person others can depend on, and who always turns up. Again, we can press this into particular categories, starting with friendship.

Friendship

Here faithfulness is seen in care and loyalty. A faithful friend is that friend who you know you can ask for help, and they won't be awkward about it, or fob you off. This is the sort of person who is always there when you need them. A very practical example of this is in dating (which is a sub-set of friendship). Faithfulness looks like honesty, in being mindful of the person's feelings, and not messing them around. To get even more granular, the faithful person keeps their word on plans, even when a 'better offer' comes along. They don't answer 'maybe' to invitations, not therefore committing in order to keep their options open. They also don't let others down when something more appealing comes up. That's selfish. Then, perhaps, most important of all, faithful friends tell their friends the truth, even when it's uncomfortable. 'You are behaving like an idiot' is something a faithful friend will say, when you are behaving like an idiot! This is why, in the book of Proverbs, it says 'faithful' are the wounds of a friend.

Marriage

Next, we have marriage. Faithfulness here is seen in physical and emotional purity: loyalty to your spouse in all things, and, in this day and age, that applies especially online. If you want to argue that watching porn, or fantasising about life with someone else, are not cheating on your spouse 'because it isn't physical', I think you're deluded. If you told your spouse about this, would they see it your way? I suggest not. Faithfulness looks like unswerving commitment to your spouse, but it also requires embracing God's design for marriage. It means embodying the role that God has given you. These roles are clearly laid out in Ephesians 5 and Colossians 3, where husbands lead the home, and wives gladly follow that lead. Husbands love their wives after the example of Christ, and wives respect their husbands. The way this plays out will look a bit different in different contexts, but faithful marriages are marked by this order. Conversely, where this order is rejected, you don't see marriages that are faithful to God.

Parenting

Another area where faithfulness will be seen is in the way parents raise their children. Faithful parents raise their children in the fear and instruction of the Lord (Eph. 6:4). They are engaged in their children's lives, teaching them the Bible, praying for them, disciplining them – just as our heavenly Father disciplines us for our good, so it is with faithful parents. We are helping prepare them for life in this world, with all of its pressures and challenges. None of us have the ability to save, or mature our children, in the faith. But that doesn't mean we shrug our shoulders and leave it to God. On occasion, I have heard people say that they don't want to meddle too much in their children's discipleship, because they 'don't want to get in God's way'. This might sound spiritual and full of faith, but it is actually nonsense. God's regular means for saving children is the instruction and prayers of their parents.

Faithful fathers will lead the home spiritually, and seek to nurture their children in the faith. If you have more than one child, this requires extra investment because one size doesn't fit all. The same parents can do the same things with each child, and they can be such different people. There's a lovely phrase in Psalm 103 describing how God the Father treats His children: 'He knows our frame; he remembers that we are dust' (v. 14).God treats us according to our frame, He knows our weakness and He knows what we can and can't take. Faithful parenting requires the same knowledge of our children.

Church

The final area I want to highlight is faithfulness in church life. This starts with a faithful leadership, like pastors who are loyal to God's word and will tell what it says even when the culture is going the other way. Then there are men who, like John Knox, fear the face of God so much they never fear the face of man. This faithfulness is the most important criteria for leaders in any church you choose to join – and where you see it you see the fruit of God's Spirit at work.

While it starts with the leaders, the fruit of faithfulness will be seen in the shared life of the church community: apparent in people who always turn up, who want jobs to do, and who are looking for ways to serve; and visible in people who block out their Sunday for the Lord and His people, investing in others, and caring for needs. Faithfulness in church sees the church as a community to join and invest in, not a service to utilise.

In the 'negative world' we're living in today the fruit of faithfulness will always be contested and challenged. Add to that the fact that our hearts are all too prone to wander from faithfulness, especially when it's costly. So we need to pray for the Lord to grow His work in us. We need also to be resolved to do what we can to enable this work, this fruit, to grow. Jesus called the church at Smyrna, in the book of Revelation, to 'Be faithful, even to the point of death …' Faithfulness would lead some of the Christians at Smyrna to death, as it does with so many across the world today. Faithfulness will inevitably cost us our reputation with some, and maybe even more with others. But here's why it is worth it: *the reward*.

In the Gospels Jesus tells a parable about a man who goes on a long journey and entrusts his property to his servants. The man is God, and the servants are people. The man gives each of them different amounts and then goes away. When he returns, he wants to see what they have done with what he has given them. He assesses things, and to those who have used well what was given he says: 'Well done, good and *faithful* servant. You have been faithful over a little; I will set you over much. Enter into the joy of your master.'

Your faithfulness *now* is the criteria by which your life will be measured on the Last Day, when you stand before God, to receive your eternal reward. As the Spirit grows faithfulness in us, we will see this kind of counter-cultural fruit. As we battle to see it grow, and live it out, even as the pressure around us rises, let us remember that it is the faithful who are welcomed into glory, and who will experience an eternity of joy.

8 Gentleness in a Time of Harshness

It wasn't so long ago that when people were losing it, it was funny. Think of the iconic *Fawlty Towers*. It's fame, legacy and quotability far outstretch the relatively few episodes that were produced. One of the central themes and causes of so much laughter was Basil's anger. Whether it was with his staff, in particular the clueless Manuel, or his customers – who can forget the lady complaining about the view from her bedroom window – or even his Austin 1100 that he famously gave a 'damn good thrashing' with the branch of a tree. If we fast forward several decades, the same idea is expressed in the 2003 film starring Jack Nicholson and Adam Sandler, called *Anger Management*. It had a plot that set out with limited success to show off the funny side of 'anger issues'.

Today we're not finding it all so funny, mainly because our world is now on fire with anger, as so much of our public discourse is angry, harsh, and full of rage. In the last chapter, I talked about how the pursuit of people online, with different views to ours, is so common. On university campuses, students protest and demand that professors are fired – their livelihood and reputation burnt to the ground – for offending them in some way or other. The theologian Scott Swain put it simply: 'we have become a culture that sees red'. And it's everywhere. Swain goes on:

> Our constant state of unhinged political outrage makes us unable to process reality, unable to determine wise courses of action, and unable to carry them through with calmness, deliberation, and justice. In our churches and homes, we also witness the consequences of untamed anger. How many [church] debates go unresolved because there are no … cool heads? How many marriages have been destroyed by wrath, quarrelling, and resentment? How many parents have traumatised their children because they cannot control their tongues …[1]

All of this, in fact, is getting increasingly normalised. Setting out to crush opponents, gloating over other peoples' failures, is just how it is. We celebrate leaders who 'crack the whip', and 'deliver results', but pass off the crushed spirits that are left in their wake as 'unfortunate, but that's life in the real world'. This kind of harshness is everywhere from the playground to the boardroom, to the church, and we've come to accept it. It doesn't have to be this way however; there is an alternative. Some will say, 'No, it's dog-eat-dog, and if you can't stick it, go home.' But, actually, what this part of Galatians 5:22-23 holds out to us is something better: the God-given gift of gentleness. If anger is the sickness, gentleness is the medicine: 'Gentleness is the spiritual virtue that tempers or moderates the desire for vengeance we experience when we suffer or witness injustice' (Scott Swain);[2] [G]entleness is 'the

---

1 Scott Swain, 'Masters of Self, Cultivating Gentleness in an Age of Outrage,' https://www.desiringgod.org/articles/masters-of-self Accessed 24.05.21.

2 Ibid.

virtue by which minds that have been rashly stirred up toward hatred of someone are restrained by kindness' (Niels Hemmingsen).[3]

Again, we see the connection between these virtues as the singular fruit of the One God, the Holy Spirit. Can you imagine the effect it would have on our culture, in your life, in your home, if the things we said and did were unmistakably marked by gentleness? It would surely be remarkable, so we need to drill down into what the Bible means when it describes this quality.

The Greek word for gentleness is similar to the word for meekness; the two are distinct. We could say gentleness is an *active trait*, describing how we should treat other people, while meekness is a *passive trait*, describing how we should respond to being badly treated by others. They are so closely related, however, we often see them used interchangeably.

Let's start by clarifying what it doesn't mean. It is important, therefore, to say that gentleness is not a personality type: strong personalities can, and must be, gentle. It is not a detached lack of emotion. Gentleness will temper emotion, not remove it. Again, it is not to be confused with niceness. Men, in particular, should not think gentleness is about becoming soft. Someone who never raises their voice, or confronts someone else, isn't necessarily gentle; they might just be a coward. Similarly, someone who stands up for what is right, and is critical of certain things, isn't necessarily arrogant or harsh. Finally, gentleness is not weakness. Jerry Bridges puts this well when he says: 'Both gentleness and meekness are born of power, not weakness. There is a pseudo-gentleness that is timidity, and there is a pseudo-meekness that is cowardly. But a Christian is to be gentle and meek [why?] because those are godlike virtues.'[4]

---

3 Ibid.
4 Bridges, p. 122.

This takes us to the heart of things. Unsurprisingly, we know what that is when we look at Jesus. So, in Matthew 11:28, we find some of the most liberating words in the Bible, when Jesus calls people to Himself saying: 'Come to me, all who labour and are heavy laden, and I will give you rest.'

The offer is rest for restless souls; an offer unmatched in its winsomeness. But then Jesus gives us a window into His own heart, in the next verses: 'Take my yoke upon you, and learn from me, for I am gentle and lowly in heart, and you will find rest for your souls. For my yoke is easy, and my burden is light.'

Dane Ortlund, in his book, *Gentle and Lowly*, points out that this is the one place in the Gospels where Jesus tells us about His own heart. He says:

> As the Son of God pulls back the veil and lets us peer way down into the core of who he is, we are not told that he is austere and demanding in heart. We are not told that he is exalted and dignified in heart. We are not even told that he is joyful and generous in heart. Letting Jesus set the terms, his surprising claim is that he is gentle and lowly in heart.'[5] This therefore means that, '[W]hen Jesus tells us what animates him most deeply, what is most true of him – when he exposes the innermost recesses of his being – what we find there is: gentle and lowly.'[6]

This is what Jesus is like. So, then, this is how Jesus *deals with* those who come to Him for rest. The writer of Hebrews says that because He is the perfect high priest, Jesus 'can deal gently with the ignorant and wayward' (5:2). That means whether your sins were foolish or wilful, accidental or intentional, Jesus will deal gently with you. This

---

5 Ortlund, *Gentle and Lowly* (Crossway, 2020), p. 19.

6 Ibid.

is good news for burdened souls like ours. The gentle and lowly heart of Christ raises His voice and turns over tables. He calls out false religion that misleads people in withering terms. He will bring lion-like judgement on those who reject Him. But to anyone who comes to Him, He receives them with gentleness:

> Jesus deals gently, and only gently with all sinners who come to him, irrespective of their particular offence and just how heinous it is. What elicits tenderness from Jesus is not the severity of the sin but whether the sinner comes to him.[7]

What this means is that if you're a Christian, this is how you have been treated, and how Jesus *goes on* treating you. When you come to Him with your sin, He isn't rough or harsh with you. He doesn't lash out; He doesn't begrudgingly say, 'Okay, fine. I suppose I said I would forgive you and I'm a man of my word.' He puts His arm around us. He deals with us according to our frame; He deals gently with us. The English puritan John Owen puts it like this: '[Jesus bears with] the infirmities, sins, and provocations of his people, even as a nurse or nursing father bears with the weakness of a poor infant.'[8]

When it comes to considering the fruit of the Spirit, therefore, that Spirit is the Spirit of Christ: this is what He is growing in us. When we are keeping in step with the Spirit (Gal. 5:25), this is the sort of lovely fruit our lives will bear. Can you imagine the effect it would have on society, if this was how growing numbers of people behaved? Also, what kind of impression might the church make, in the midst of so much ugly anger and harshness, if this was how her members behaved?

---

7   Ibid., p. 54.
8   Owen, quoted in Ortlund, p. 55.

GENTLE JESUS

The problem in the church is that so many of us have forgotten how Jesus has treated us. We see how this works out, in the parable of the unforgiving servant in Matthew 18. In the story the servant owed the king a fortune. He was in massive debt and he sought the king's mercy. The king responded with gentleness, and forgave him and let him go free. But the servant then went out to another servant, who owed him a much smaller amount, and demanded he pay, putting him in prison until he could. Jesus tells the parable to make the point that God is *so* merciful. He is gentle with us to *such* a degree, that for us not to have this posture towards others, is out of step with knowing Him.

If you take a moment to think about your life, call to mind the secret sins you've coddled – the small sins as well as the bigger sins. Next, think about the law's demands for perfect obedience. Then consider about how Jesus has dealt with you. He has been gentle, not giving you what you deserve, but instead giving you grace and mercy. Think over how ungrateful and impetuous we so often are, because we haven't got what we want. Consider just how we've become hard to God, and grown cold to His mercy and grace, because the life we want isn't the one He has given us. How has Jesus dealt with us? He has been gentle, sustaining us and ensuring we keep going, getting us another step along the path to glory. Like the unforgiving servant we have short memories, and so we get angry at others. We are harsh with our children, and we lash out when we feel wronged. We need to repent of that – but when we do, what will we find? We will meet Jesus and find that He is gentle with us, and will forgive us.

GRACIOUS JESUS

But we haven't just forgotten how Jesus has treated us; we've also forgotten what He has given us. By that I mean that we have forgotten the benefits of knowing Jesus. In Christ, God accepts you. He loves you, values and dignifies you. This means that you don't need to put others down, or show you're better than them in some way in order to be accepted – or to be someone. There is so much anger and conflict flowing from our insecurity, along with a related desire to prove ourselves to be 'somebody'. Competitiveness is a very good thing: it is vital in sport or in combat, but it's no good at all in a marriage, a friendship, or in church life. When you've been accepted by God, you don't need to feel threatened by your younger colleague's ability, such that you put them down. You don't need to dominate in any given setting, you don't need to be in control, and you don't need to win every argument. You also don't need to right every wrong against you. God knows the truth and will vindicate you in the end. In the same way, you don't need to have everything you want, because God cares for you, and He will provide. What all of this means is that the grace of Christ that comes to us in the gospel enables us to be gentle.

If you were trying to drum up security and peace in your own strength, you will fail a hundred times out of a hundred. If you remember who you now are in Christ, however, and walk in step with His Spirit at work in you, gentleness will flow through all your dealings with others. Here are five ways you will see gentleness in your life:

1. *You actively seek to put people at ease in your company.* Whether in the workplace, and you are senior to them, or in other peer relationships, you help people to feel they can be themselves without fear. Especially where you are in authority over someone, or you have the power in the relationship dynamic, gentleness sees the other person and seeks to put them at ease.

2. *You are slow to take offence.* Gentleness grows in the company of humility. Scott Swain again puts it well when he says: 'Proud, self-important people are easily angered, easily offended. When they do not receive the respect they deserve (or think they deserve …), when their opinions are not validated, when their advice is not heeded, they rage, they resent, they seek revenge.'[9] Humble (gospel) people, however, aren't like this, because of what we've said about what Jesus has given us. Humble people 'recognise that their true dignity is both given and guarded by God, when they are wronged, they entrust vengeance to God and pursue the path of forgiveness and reconciliation with their neighbours. Because they know that God will maintain their cause, they are free from having to maintain their own cause, and they are free to devote themselves to God's cause and to the cause of their neighbours. Indeed, only the meek are truly qualified to pursue the cause of truth and righteousness.'[10]

3. *You are careful with words.* 'A gentle answer turns away wrath, but a harsh word stirs up anger.'[11] Gentleness avoids being harsh and abrupt. This is an area where Christians from my tradition fall down. We care about truth and being right and so that's where the emphasis in lots of our communication lands, rather than caring about how what we say is heard. This is definitely a work-on for me. My wife often tells me that 'just because something is true doesn't mean it needs to be said'.

4. *You are humane towards opponents.* Gentleness demands that we dignify those who we disagree with, or who have treated us

---

9   https://www.desiringgod.org/articles/masters-of-self
10   Ibid.
11   Proverbs 15.1 (NIV).

badly. At the very least, this means we see them as fellow image-bearers of God. It is easy to de-humanise opponents, but the fruit of gentleness won't allow this. In debate, therefore, we seek to maintain the relationship even where our disagreements are serious. In conflict, we hold back, rather than trying to make them suffer like we are suffering. Gentleness tempers our anger and holds us back from seeking revenge, even in the face of injustice.

5. *You are considerate towards those who fail.* Our culture loves us to gloat over another person's failure – it's another way of shoring up our own insecurities. We assume a posture that thinks, for now at least, that person is worse than me, and I can take a kind of perverse comfort in that. But that's a foolish way to think, and a toxic way to live. It is better to be gentle: to accept that they could just as easily have been you, and seek to help restore them. In the life of the church when someone falls into sin, the gentle person is grieved, and will pray for them, rather than looking down on them, or talking about them to others. When you have failed, you feel condemned. So being met with such gentleness is a life-giving and hopeful thing. This shouldn't be a surprise because, as we've seen, that's the way of Jesus.

As always, there will be more ways that gentleness quietly and humbly manifests in the life of those who walk in step with the Spirit. These, however, are five obvious examples, and where you see these qualities in your life, praise God, who gives this fruit as a gift. Where it is absent, go to the source, and ask for it. Jesus possesses a reservoir of gentleness that never runs dry; a reservoir that, by His Spirit, we can draw freely from, over and over again, and we must. So, go to Him, and there you will find not only rest for your soul, but the only balm that will heal an angry world.

9 Self-Control in a Time of Self-Obsession

Self-control …

I imagine some will read those words and think: 'All right, I know what's coming. This is the church's sweet spot. Look around at this greedy and dissolute culture; the ugly excesses everywhere. Don't be like that. Get your life under control.' That's a common view of the kind of message the church has to offer these days. 'Drum up the resolve, and go and be more morally upright' is the kind of thing. This is almost as out of step with the current culture as the supposedly regressive views that I mentioned in chapter 7. Why would anybody think that trying to be self-controlled is a good idea? Surely the whole point of life is to go after whatever you can get, and enjoy it as much as possible? I am taught to believe that life is a blank canvas for me to paint on whatever I want, so why would I say 'no' to anything? In fact, the Bible doesn't actually tell us to 'go and try hard to be moral'. Indeed, 'try harder' is actually the opposite of the Christian good news. What is interesting, however, is that it's a message that's very popular in our culture at the moment.

Whether it's Jordan Peterson's *12 Rules*, Joe Wicks' diet and exercise plan, or one of the thousands of online, life-change specialists – emotional, physical, spiritual, professional – the message is basically the same: 'Go and make yourself the better version of you, that you want to be …' In every single case, this involves a measure of self-control. You will be told to stop doing something, and to start doing something else. Both of these require self-control. Self-control is big business at the moment.

There is lots that is good about this. Jordan Peterson has not become a global hero to many because his lists of rules don't actually have an effect on people's lives. Willpower *can* get you well down the road to career success, or to personal life-change. During the lockdowns of 2020, alongside the job loss stories, there were stories of start-up success online. For everyone who let themselves go, there was a successful transformation story to match. In each case, discipline and self-denial make it happen. Then, of course, things like shame, guilt, and the praise of others, are all powerful motivators to take control of your life. All of these factors play a part in motivating people all the way to the top of their field.

In his memoir, the former England rugby-union captain, Dylan Hartley, talked at length about what playing at the top level of the game required of him: 'self-imposed disciplines became draining, because they eventually bordered on the illogical. They were all I thought about, first thing in the morning and last thing at night. The moment I opened my eyes, I instinctively gauged how I was feeling. I worried about what I would eat for breakfast. Forget a fry-up – I denied myself a slice of toast, because I knew it would have a knock-on effect. Aware that the horror of my indulgence would be revealed in the weekly skin fold test, I became fixated …'[1]

Lots of people manage their lives with varying degrees of self-control, and that's fine and good as far as it goes. But where our self-control is for the sake of ourselves – our body image, our career advancement, our achievement – it isn't the sort of self-control that the Spirit creates; even where we do this in a religious way. Again, it's the popular view of Christianity: a religion about, 'don't do this, that, or the other and that will please God'. That's just as off the mark as any other expression of self-control. In his letter to the Colossians, the Apostle Paul rebukes the church for embracing this kind of idea:

> If with Christ you died to the elemental spirits of the world, why, as if you were still alive in the world, do you submit to regulations – 'Do not handle, Do not taste, Do not touch' (referring to things that all perish as they are used) – according to human precepts and teachings? These have indeed an appearance of wisdom in promoting self-made religion and asceticism and severity to the body, but they are of no value in stopping the indulgence of the flesh (Col. 2:20-23).

Self-made religion, asceticism, and severity to the body, will not bring your heart under control. Our instinct is to squirm when we hear the mention of self-control, because we know that there are areas of our life that we haven't been able to master. But don't think that self-made religion, with its regulations and rituals, is the answer. It isn't, because it can only deal with externals; it can't get to the heart.

The self-control the Spirit cultivates, works from the inside out. It starts with the heart, and it has pleasing God as its goal. We can define this kind of self-control as: mastery of our heart in order that

---

1   Dylan Hartley, *The Hurt* (Viking, 2020), p. 8.

our lives please God. This mastery is what the Spirit gives us – deep personal transformation, the sort we can't work up on our own. The word, 'self-control', that Paul uses in the list in Galatians 5:22-23 refers to the moderation or tempering of our desires and appetites. Literally it could mean 'inner strength' and 'refers to that strength of character that enables one to control his or her passions and desires'.[2]

The focus here is on the heart, but because the heart is the source of our behaviour – this is the theology of the book of Proverbs: 'above all else guard your heart for it is the wellspring of life' (4:23) – when we master our hearts, we master our lives. Now, as we've said throughout this book, the fruit of the Spirit is not a new law. Paul is not telling the Galatian church to go and do these things. He is saying that these are the qualities that the Spirit works in those who follow Christ. We 'crucify our flesh' (see Gal. 5:24) and 'keep in step with the Spirit' (see 5:25), so we do what we can to help cultivate the Spirit's work in our lives; but this is God's work in us. So if we profess to follow Jesus, these things will be evident to some degree, and they will be growing. The goal of a short book like this one, therefore, is to highlight what we are looking out for. When it comes to self-control, mastery of the heart and life will be seen in how we handle our thoughts, our desires and our actions.

OUR THOUGHTS

In his book, *With All Your Heart*,[3] Craig Troxel points out how, when the Bible talks about the heart, it can mean our mind, our desires, or our will. So, we need to start with our thoughts. Self-control is often linked with 'sober-mindedness' (1 Tim. 3:2; Titus 1:8; 2:2). Our minds are like greenhouses that grow all kinds of thoughts, some of which

---

2   Bridges, p. 133.

3   Craig Troxel, *With All Your Heart* (Crossway, 2020).

aren't very pleasant. If these thoughts are left to grow unchecked, if they are not mastered by the Spirit at work in us, they won't just stay in our heads. They will grow out into our actions. No one just falls into serious sin, like no one just falls off a cliff. If you're nowhere near the edge, you don't fall. It's the same with sin. The reason we fall is that we have allowed our thoughts to run and run. We have entertained and enjoyed the fantasy in our minds, and, before we know it, we're at the cliff's edge, and over we go.

Speaking down to someone in a proud and condescending way doesn't just happen; it starts with you thinking you're better than them. Self-pity and discontentment don't just happen; it starts with thinking you deserve better than you have. Every case of adultery could have been prevented if the initial idea had been 'taken captive' (Paul's language in 2 Corinthians) and rejected. A self-controlled mind is the first line of defence in a self-controlled life. It requires us to take hold of the ungodly and destructive thoughts at the earliest moment. As soon as we are aware that our minds are going down a destructive track, we stop. But, as with all these things, we can't just stop thinking about something in a vacuum. If I tell you now to stop thinking about brown bears, you can't!

We need to shift our thinking to something else, something that is pleasing to God. Paul says in Philippians 4:8 that 'whatever is true, whatever is honourable, whatever is just, whatever is pure, whatever is lovely, whatever is commendable, if there is any excellence, if there is anything worthy of praise, think about these things.' And I want to highlight Paul's emphasis on truth (and rightness) here, because I think this is an area where lots of our thinking lacks self-control. In Romans 12 Paul tells us that Christian thinking involves our minds not being conformed to the world, but being transformed by the renewing of our minds, in order to discern what God wants. This means our thinking is to be governed by the Bible, not the culture, nor our emotions, nor the opinions of the cool-crowd. Singleness, marriage roles, work, gender, and sexuality are all areas of life where lots of people in the contemporary church have lost their way – because their thinking has drifted from the Bible.

OUR DESIRES

Closely linked to our thoughts, a second area where self-control will be seen, is in our desires. That means we will have mastery over what we love; we will control the things that our heart goes after. We won't indulge in lust, cultivating sexual desire for someone we shouldn't. Just to clarify for our loophole-seeking minds: if you're single, that's anyone; if you're married, that's anyone apart from your spouse. Self-control will keep us from pornography, or from anything else that will even encourage this misplaced desire. Perhaps less obvious, but equally destructive, we won't indulge desires for the easy life. Some of us long for the good life according to the world's categories – the house, the holidays, the Instagram vision of happiness and ease. That is not in step with the cross-shaped path that Jesus calls us to, in following Him. We do nothing to check those desires. In fact, we positively encourage them with the things we look at, and the comparisons we draw with others. Self-control is seen when we master those desires, such that our vision of the good life is in line with what pleases God. Don't mishear me. In 1 Timothy 6:12 we are told that God gives us all that we have to enjoy. He is a Father who loves to give good gifts and He doesn't give them with a teaspoon. He is generous beyond belief. But self-controlled desires can enjoy those gifts without them controlling us, so without us *needing* them. A gift stops being a gift, if it becomes a master, and self-control is what determines the difference.

OUR ACTIONS

Self-controlled thoughts and desires, then, will lead to a self-controlled life and self-controlled actions. This will draw in all the obvious areas, *our appetites*: what we do with food, drink and sex. Self-control keeps these in check. We enjoy food without it becoming something we can't resist, or we go to for comfort. We enjoy alcohol in the same way. Alcohol is something that the Bible says we are free to enjoy. But if we can't moderate our intake, it has ceased to be a freedom – we are no longer free, but enslaved. Self-control enables us to enjoy it in a way that honours God. It is the same with sex; self-control is what keeps sex within the framework that God designed for our flourishing.

Other obvious areas are those like our *speech*: self-control uses words carefully. It restrains our desire to say what we might think, but we know would do harm. In the area of *laziness*, self-control manages time well, and isn't wasteful with it. It restrains the desire to mindlessly binge-watch Netflix, and to disappear into computer games. It gets you up early to spend time with the Lord, to pray for yourself, your family, your church, and God's mission in the world. In the area of *aggression*, we need self-control to channel it into healthy things like hard work and exercise and protecting the vulnerable, and not allow it to overflow into conflict or violence.

You might think of more areas, but where I think this quality is seen most clearly is in how it plays out in this list that Paul gives in Galatians 5:22-23. I don't think self-control is just the last thing that Paul, under the inspiration of the Spirit, thought of when he described the work that same Spirit does in the Christian believer. Self-control is connected to the other aspects as the means by which we can see them grow in our lives. Self-control is what restrains your hatred so that you love. It is what restrains your grumpiness and discontent so that you know joy. Self-control is what prevents you from growing restless so that you enjoy the peace of God. It's what restrains your impatience, cultivating patience. Self-control resists selfishness and enables you to bear the fruit of kindness and goodness. It is what holds back the desire to follow the crowd away from God in order to bear the fruit of faithfulness. It is also self-control that keeps anger in check, so that your life is marked by gentleness.

Self-control enables us to resist the temptation for self-promotion, self-glory, or self-indulgence, therefore to know the freedom that this brings. That is what He offers us.

The self-discipline that's increasingly popular in the culture today is always going to be limited in time, because we can't keep it going. Dylan Hartley's point was that he simply couldn't get himself either emotionally or physically to where he needed to be, so he had to retire. The same is true in scope; that is, we can get one area of life under control, but the others keep on running away from us. When this happens, it is very frustrating. We feel so feeble because our appetites have won out again, and we think, 'Why can't I just say "no"?!' This is especially true when we look around us and see other people who seem to have everything together. The self-control, however, that the Spirit grows in those who trust Jesus, is all-encompassing, because it comes from the heart. The Spirit works to change the source.

If you think about a polluted river, the only way the water downstream will change is if the cause of the problem upstream is dealt with. The source of our problems is our heart. Until that is changed, however hard we try, we will still have the problems. But when our hearts are changed by the Spirit, all this fruit starts to grow; this is the clean water.

What this then means is, that what we're talking about is good news. Far from being another 'go and be a good person' message, the kind of self-mastery we need is something that we are actually given in Jesus Christ. Christian self-control is not finally about bringing our hearts and lives under our own control, but under the control of Christ, by walking in step with His Spirit. So we give ourselves to Him. He is the vine and we are the branches. As we do this, He will grow this fruit in us, and our lives won't just please God – they will be marked by freedom and joy.

Conclusion

Don't you want this life?

As I reflect on these short chapters I find myself wishing my life would bear the Spirit's fruit in greater abundance. I long to grow in all of these beautiful qualities because I know that it will make me a better, more contented person. It is also obvious that I would be a better husband, father, friend, and citizen if my life was marked more deeply by this work. Can you imagine the sort of society we would create if more people knew the reality of God's Spirit in their lives? If your local community was full of people who chose to love others rather than look out for themselves; if the drivers on your roads were peaceful at the wheel and patient with other road users; if your local council was marked by kindness and goodness, it would be a delightful place to live. An obvious question we therefore need to ask is how can we get, and grow, this fruit in our lives?

Just as you can't stand in front of an apple tree and tell it to grow apples, you can't tell yourself (or someone else) to grow spiritual fruit. As you desire to bear this fruit you need to accept that you are not the main cause of change in your life. Paul's language is passive (Gal. 5:18): we 'are led by the Spirit'. As I have emphasised throughout this book, the qualities that Paul describes are not a law or a standard to be attained; they are the 'fruit' of another's work in us. They are produced because the Spirit is giving us spiritual life. But because we are the recipients of this supernatural work, doesn't mean that we are left with nothing to do. We Christians don't simply sit on our hands waiting for God to change us: Paul also includes an active image (5:16) where we 'walk by the Spirit' and (5:25, Christian Standard Bible) 'keep in step with the Spirit'. It's not that we make the Spirit work, He is already at work, but that we line up with Him. He is moving in the world, bringing God's purposes to pass, and we need to match our step to His. If we change the image to that of a canoeist in a fast-flowing river, we see he has a canoe and a paddle that are for the express purpose of getting himself into the current. That is how he will get to where he wants to go. He can't change what the river is doing – he gets into what it is already doing, and goes where it takes him. So how do we get the canoe of our lives into the Spirit's fast-flowing current?

DIE TO SELF

The first thing we need to recognise is what we saw right back in the first chapter where we have to crucify our flesh with its passions and desires (see Gal. 5:24). The desires of the flesh are the basic instincts that we are born with, and that we naturally live out of. We don't need to be taught or instructed how to live this way, because they are the default setting of every human life. The desires of the flesh are, therefore, against the Spirit and they simply will not play nicely together. This means that if the Spirit will grow His fruit in our lives, we have to go to war.

Tim Chester puts it well when he says: 'We're to oppose the murderous intent of the flesh with murderous intent … The flesh is trying to kill us, so we kill the flesh.'[1] This means we fight to flee the temptations that so naturally rise up within us. This won't just be temptation towards the obvious vices in our world, but also the temptation to live in a way that contradicts the Spirit's work. This will mean fighting to resist a critical word that doesn't demonstrate love. It will mean fighting that grumbling spirit that is the antithesis of joy, or the anger that rises up to rob us of our peace. There are lots of ways that Christians indulge what I have heard called 'respectable sins', often without realising. These need to be resisted and repented of, if the Spirit's fruit will grow. This is the battle of the Christian life, and it is one that we must engage if our lives will move in the direction the Spirit is going.

MEANS OF GRACE

Negatively, we must die to ourselves and our appetites. God, however, has also given us things to positively pursue, through which He does His work. If the Spirit is the river, God also gives us the canoe, the paddle, and any other equipment we need to help us to get into the current. These are what are known as the means of grace; that is, the means through which God works to accomplish His intended ends for our lives.

GOD'S WORD

The first of the means of grace is God's word. God spoke the world into being, and it is His word that also brings salvation. The Apostle

---

1 Tim Chester, *Rediscovering Joy* (IVP, 2017), p. 80.

brings these two together in 2 Corinthians 4:6. 'For God, who said, "Let light shine out of darkness," has shone in our hearts to give the light of the knowledge of the glory of God in the face of Jesus Christ.' Both creation and redemption come about through the power of God speaking. He has breathed out this word in the Holy Scriptures (2 Tim. 3:16) so that we can know Him and know how we should live in His world. This means that if we want to know His power in our lives we need to listen to the Bible.

When you read the Bible God speaks: He shines a light on our sin; He shows us our Saviour; He encourages us to persevere – and the Holy Spirit applies what He says to our lives in order to change us and bring out His fruit. We should say that while the word of God will always do us good – whenever and wherever we read or study it – it is especially powerful when it is preached in the midst of the gathered church. In God's design, when qualified men proclaim His word faithfully on the Lord's Day, the same power that breathed the cosmos into being is unleashed among His people. Giving ourselves to God's word, listening attentively to His voice – particularly making sure we hear it preached, with the church – will lead us to walk more closely in step with the Spirit.

PRAYER

The second means that God uses is the other side of this relationship, namely prayer. If He speaks in His word, we respond in prayer – and just like in any relationship, this is a vital element in the deepening of our communion. Prayer is an opportunity to draw near to God – as through the finished work and ongoing ministry of Christ, our great High Priest – we are welcome in His presence. Not only that, as Romans 8:26-27 makes clear, when we speak, even when we don't have the right words, the Holy Spirit intercedes on our behalf to perfect our prayers. In this way, prayer is a trinitarian pursuit through which we don't simply praise God for who He is, or thank Him for all that He has done for us. But we also seek His strength and enabling to resist temptation, to crucify our flesh, and grow in the fruit of the Spirit.

If we want to pursue the Spirit's work in our lives, we simply must pray. There is no hope of growth without it. Too many of us allow our activism to choke the Spirit's work in our lives because we are too busy doing things *for* God to spend the time *with* God – time that is needed to see His fruit borne in our lives. In many ways, it feels like we are trying to get into the fast-flowing current without getting into the canoe! God has given us this means of His grace, but we leave it to the side, trying instead to do things in our own strength. When we struggle with sin, prayer is how we repent, how we gain strength, how we grow a desire for holiness, so we find sin less appealing next time. Prayer is how we express our desire for greater godliness, in order that God might answer. Prayer is vital if we will see the fruit of God's Spirit grow.

THE SACRAMENTS

Finally, because God gives His gifts with a ladle and not a teaspoon, there is also grace for His people, in what has been called through church history, the sacraments. God therefore doesn't just speak in His word, but He also speaks to us in water, bread and wine – the sacraments of baptism and the Lord's Supper. These are signs of God's covenant, His promise to His people, and so they speak to us of our belonging both to Him, and to the community of His people: the church. In baptism – death, resurrection, cleansing and new life are symbolised – as the gospel of God's free grace is visibly proclaimed. Likewise, the Lord's Supper preaches the same gospel.

In the broken bread and shared wine, we see and participate in the broken body and shed blood of Christ (1 Cor. 10:16), through which our redemption has been won. God didn't design baptism or the Lord's Supper to have any intrinsic power. These sacraments are not intended to function by themselves, but rather they function as signs and seals of the promise of the gospel. J. V. Fesko describes how we experience the sacraments like this:

> God uses word and sacrament to preach not merely to our minds and hearts, but to all of our senses. We hear the word of God with our ears and we see the word of God with our eyes when we observe a baptism. We feel the word of God when we receive the water of baptism. And we can even say that we taste and smell the word of God when we partake of the bread and wine. In effect, God preaches the gospel to all our senses, which is a reminder that we will be wholly redeemed, body and soul.[2]

When you are baptised, you are baptised into the community of the Spirit. When you eat bread and drink the cup with the Lord's people, you participate in Christ, the man of the Spirit. There are evangelical churches where these gifts from God for our growth in grace are often, sadly, downplayed. Baptism may be reduced to a mere visible sign of something God has done in the believer's heart. The Lord's Supper might be celebrated rarely, and in a diminished way. The sacraments, however, that the Lord has given us are given for our spiritual nourishment. They help us grow in grace and manifest the fruit of the Spirit.

God's Word, prayer and the sacraments of baptism and the Lord's Supper are the appointed means that God uses to give us His grace. They get us off the riverbank and into the fast- flowing current, they

---

2   J. V. Fesko, *The Fruit of The Spirit Is* (Evangelical Press, 2011), p. 63.

get us up and walking, in step with the Spirit, in order that we can live the kind of fruitful life that we've been considering in this book.

In closing, I want to point out an encouragement that we can easily forget, and that is the inevitability of success. What I mean is that few of us feel like getting out of bed each day and putting our 'Winner' hat on. Our battle with the desires of the flesh rarely feels like it is going well. But because bearing spiritual fruit is ultimately the work of the Spirit, He will accomplish it. A day is coming when the struggle will come to an end. We will have been led by the Spirit to glory, to the new heavens and new earth, and God will see to it that we get there. Therefore, put your hope in God the Father, rest in the work of Christ the Son, and walk on in step with the Spirit, for that is the good life.

THE LIES WE ARE TOLD, THE TRUTH WE MUST HOLD

Worldviews and Their Consequences

SHARON JAMES

The Lies We Are Told, The Truth We Must Hold

Worldviews and Their Consequences

Sharon James

We are surrounded by lies. They are incorporated into the worldview of our culture. We daily absorb them, and these lies can have deadly effects on individuals, societies and whole civilisations.

Sharon James investigates the origins of some of these lies and looks at how we have got to the point where 'my truth' is as valid as 'your truth', and absolute truth is an outdated way of thinking. In examining the evidence of history, she highlights the consequences of applying dangerous untruths. She also looks at how Christians often respond to the culture's lies – in silence, acquiescence or celebration of them – and why these responses can be as harmful as the lies themselves.

In the second part she turns to the truth which leads to real liberation and justice. She shows why we don't need to be ashamed of Christ, or intimidated by the claims of those who are militantly opposed to the Bible.

… a remarkable feat: she addresses the lies that our culture currently exalts as truth and does so in a way that crosses the generational divide and will be helpful both to young people and those who wish to understand them and help them think through the deepest challenges of our day.

Carl R. Trueman
Professor of Biblical and Religious Studies, Grove City College,
Pennsylvania

978-1-5271-0796-0

DAVID A. SMITH

HIDDEN AGENDAS

Demands of the heart that
stop us loving God and others

Hidden Agendas

Demands of the Heart that Stop Us Loving God and Others

David A. Smith

This book lifts the lid on the human heart, seeking to uncover the hidden agendas that stop us from loving God and others as we should. Our hearts have a selfish list of priorities that we believe are important and need to be given attention. But often these heart agendas are in tension with God's agenda.

David Smith uses four biblical pictures to help us consider these agendas that are often hidden so deep within our hearts that we are unaware of them. Using examples from the Bible, he uncovers the desire to be significant; the desire to have certainty; the desire to have peace, safety, and security; and the desire for our own fulfilment.

This book is a perceptive analysis using four biblical passages of the hidden agendas that can lurk in each human heart. With appropriate and often deeply moving pastoral insights from his own life and refreshing honesty, the author reveals these agendas and the corresponding heart problems they generate. I thoroughly recommend it as a book to strengthen our confidence in the adequacy of God.

John Lennox
Professor of Mathematics, University of Oxford, Fellow in Mathematics and Philosophy of Science, Green Templeton College

978-1-5271-0836-3

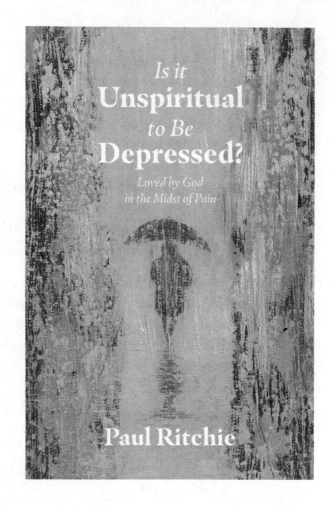

Is it
Unspiritual
to Be
Depressed?

Loved by God
in the Midst of Pain

Paul Ritchie

Is It Unspiritual to Be Depressed?
Loved by God in the Midst of Pain
Paul Ritchie

Writing from his own experience as a pastor who has struggled with depression, anxiety and O.C.D., Paul Ritchie addresses some of the big questions that Christians with mental illnesses and those around them might ask. Although he deals frankly with the reality of mental illness in a fallen world, he shows how the gospel is good news for those suffering. He applies the truth of the gospel, assuring readers that they can take God at His word, even when their brain tells them to doubt. His final chapter also gives helpful advice for those who want to help friends or family who are depressed or anxious.

Written with grace, wisdom, and from personal experience, the book will carefully and gently help readers navigate some difficult pastoral issues relating to mental health.

Peter Orr

Lecturer in New Testament, Moore Theological College, Sydney

There are books addressing depression from a clinical, personal or spiritual perspective. What sets this one apart is the fact that it addresses the issue from all three perspectives. You will be challenged by Paul's honesty, his empathy for others and his ceaseless focus on the Gospel. In fact, you will never think about the issue the same way again.

David Blevin

Sky News

978-1-5271-0789-2

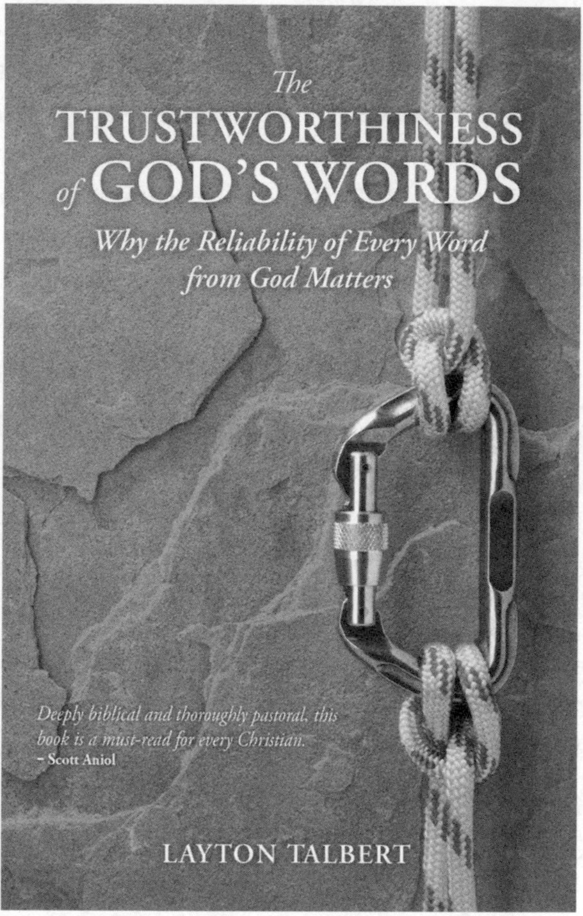
The
TRUSTWORTHINESS
of GOD'S WORDS
Why the Reliability of Every Word from God Matters
Deeply biblical and thoroughly pastoral, this book is a must-read for every Christian.
– Scott Aniol
LAYTON TALBERT

The Trustworthiness of God's Words

Why the Reliability of Every Word from God Matters

Layton Talbert

This is a book about God's jealousy for His integrity, His passion to be believed, on the basis of His words alone. Throughout Scripture God expresses His determination to be known as the God who keeps His words. Learning to trust a God who is sovereign and in control, especially in the ache and throb of life, means hanging on to the conviction that everything He says is utterly dependable.

Layton Talbert demonstrates from God's own words that God is passionate about vindicating the complete integrity and trustworthiness of his words. All of God's words are reliable. God always keeps his words.

Andy Naselli
Associate Professor of New Testament and Systematic Theology, Bethlehem College and Seminary, Minneapolis, Minnesota

Layton Talbert explains clearly, and in an engaging way, that if we do believe what God says, we bring glory to Him; and we enjoy the confidence in his sovereignty that enables us to 'laugh at the days to come' (Proverbs 31:25).

Sharon James
Social Policy Analyst, The Christian Institute

978-1-5271-0790-8

Rich Grace
IN POOR SOIL

GROWING IN THE MASTER'S GRIP

Kenneth B. Wingate

Rich Grace in Poor Soil

Growing in the Master's Grip

Kenneth B. Wingate

The garden provides the perfect image for the work of grace in our lives. In fact, Scripture often uses plant–based metaphors to describe the life of the believer. From the planting of the gospel seed to growing into oaks of righteousness, Kenneth Wingate explores these different aspects to show how we can flourish in Christ and bear fruit for Him.

Rich Grace in Poor Soil *leads you to the very heart of God. For anyone who feels bruised, hurt or worn out, this book will refresh the soul. Written with a sharpness of insight and a flair for illustration, Rich Grace in Poor Soil is a tonic.*

Derek W. H. Thomas
Senior Minister of Preaching and Teaching, First Presbyterian Church, Columbia, South Carolina

Ken Wingate wants you to wallow in grace. In this manual for the Christian life he writes of deep grace with such a light touch—and good sense. Insights abound; the book is simply fun to read.

Dale Ralph Davis
Respected Author and Old Testament Scholar

978-1-5271-0806-6

Christian Focus Publications

Our mission statement –

STAYING FAITHFUL
In dependence upon God we seek to impact the world through
literature faithful to His infallible Word, the Bible. Our aim is
to ensure that the Lord Jesus Christ is presented as the only hope
to obtain forgiveness of sin, live a useful life and look forward to
heaven with Him.

Our books are published in four imprints:

CHRISTIAN
FOCUS

Popular works including biographies,
commentaries, basic doctrine and
Christian living.

CHRISTIAN
HERITAGE

Books representing some of
the best material from the rich
heritage of the church.

MENTOR

Books written at a level suitable
for Bible College and seminary
students, pastors, and other serious
readers. The imprint includes
commentaries, doctrinal studies,
examination of current issues and
church history.

CF4•K

Children's books for quality Bible
teaching and for all age groups:
Sunday school curriculum, puzzle and
activity books; personal and family
devotional titles, biographies and
inspirational stories – because you are
never too young to know Jesus!

Christian Focus Publications Ltd,
Geanies House, Fearn, Ross-shire,
IV20 1TW, Scotland, United Kingdom.
www.christianfocus.com
blog.christianfocus.com